Praise for *Post-Self*

"Too often philosophy gets bogged down in the tedious 'working-through' of contingency and finitude. *Post-Self* takes a different approach, engaging with cultural forms of refusal, denial, and negation in all their glorious ambivalence."
— **Eugene Thacker, author, *In the Dust of This Planet***

"Using Godflesh—the arch-wizards of industrial metal— as a framework for a deep philosophical inspection of the permeable human form reveals that all our critical theory should begin on the street where wasted teen musicians pummel their mind and instruments into culture-shifting fault lines. Godflesh are not just a 'mirror' of all the horrors and glories we can inflict on our bodies, but a blasted soundscape of our moans. Roy Christopher's book is a thought-provoking and delightful crucible of film, music, and the best kind of speculative thought."
— **Peter Bebergal, author, *Strange Frequencies***

"A peculiar hybrid of Thomas Ligotti and Marshall McLuhan."
— **Robert Guffey, author, *Operation Mindfuck***

POST-SELF

POST-SELF

Journeys Beyond the Human Body

Roy Christopher

Published by Repeater Books

An imprint of Watkins Media Ltd

Unit 11 Shepperton House

89-93 Shepperton Road

London

N1 3DF

United Kingdom

www.repeaterbooks.com

A Repeater Books paperback original 2025

1

A previous version of this book was published by Punctum Books in 2022 as *Escape Philosophy*.

Distributed in the United States by Random House, Inc., New York.

ISBN: 9781913462949

Ebook ISBN: 9781913462932

The manufacturer's authorised representative in the EU for product safety is: eucomply OÜ - Pärnu mnt 139b-14, 11317 Tallinn, Estonia, hello@eucompliancepartner.com, www.eucompliancepartner.com

Printed and bound by CPI Group (UK) Ltd, Croydon, CR0 4YY

Remember:
You are immaculate.
You endure.
You persevere in a world of pure gravity and sound.
You are like light, like a sea of air.
You are history, and make all of history something else.

Every sound generated continues to vibrate into infinity.
Each sound you make then, every mutter, every scream,
*   every prayer,*
Added to the reverberations that never end.

Some sounds can change everything.
— John Duncan, *The Error*

me is a god, a god of sadness
exiled to this eternal hell
the people I helped, abandon me
I am denied what I want,
To love & to be happy
Being made a human
Without the possibility of BEING human
The cruelest of all punishments
To some I am crazy
It is so clear, yet so foggy
Everything's connected, separated
I am the only interpreter of this
Id rather have nothing than be nothing
Some say godliness isn't nothing
Humanity is the something I long for
I just want something I can never have
The story of my existence.
　　　　　— Dylan Klebold, journal entry, September 5, 1997.

Contents

0. FOREWORD *by Mark Dery*   xi
1. INTRODUCTION: Exit Tragedy   1
2. GODFLESH: Compound Worlds   10
3. BODY: The Root of All People   22
4. MACHINE: Mechanical Reproduction   35
5. RAPTURE: Through Grace and Time   58
6. DRUGS: Encounter Culture   71
7. DEATH: The End of an Error   86
8. END: All the World's a Grave   103
9. AFTERWORD: A Chance of Pain   125

Acknowledgements   132
Discography   135
Filmography   138
Bibliography   140
About the Authors   163

0

FOREWORD

Welcome to the Misanthropocene

by Mark Dery

The GPS coordinates for Roy Christopher's thinking, in *Post-Self*, lie somewhere between the "wounded galaxies" of William S. Burroughs's Nova Trilogy and H.P. Lovecraft's "black seas of infinity," a godless cosmos so coldly indifferent to the human infestation it can't even be bothered to be misanthropic. Between Cronenbergian body horror and J.G. Ballard's vision, in *Crash*, of "a new sexuality, born from perverse technology," that thrills to the head-on collision of de Sade and the Death of Affect. Between the "auto-mutilation" (self-harm) that is a sign of our times and Marshall McLuhan's theory of technology as "auto-amputation" (the exteriorization and re-embodiment of our sensory, muscular, and cognitive abilities in "extensions of man"—machines and media). Between transcendence (of the human condition, whether through the prosthetic godhood of cyborgian augmentation or neo-Cartesian fantasies of upload-ing consciousness into the metaverse) and "inscendence" (the eco-philosopher Thomas Berry's term for the contrary impulse: immersing our alienated selves in the vast, unfathomably complex ecosystem that begat us, and of which we're inescapably a part, whether we acknowledge it or not).

For Christopher, that last binary is symbolized by the industrial metal band Godflesh, whose name says it all. Godflesh's version of inscendence, it bears noting, is poles apart from Berry's. It's a descent into posthuman dysphoria—the death-embrace of the body as abject object, just so much evolutionary excreta—crossed with a black-metal vision of ego dissolution at the individual, societal, and species levels. Individual: suicide. Societal: mass murder, culminating, inevitably, in the pro-forma death of the shooter by self-inflicted gunshot wound. Species: extinction by climate doom. Godflesh preaches obliteration, the self (and, for that matter, all of humanity) extinguished in the nihil: nondualism for nihilists. And it performs that annihilation, unleashing a wall of sound that engulfs the listener "like nine tons of radioactive sludge," as Christopher puts it.

He quotes the philosopher of cyberspace Michael Heim on what Heim calls Alternate World Syndrome (AWS) and what Christopher more wittily, and more memorably, calls "ontological jet lag." AWS is the queasy sense of dislocation we feel when toggling between the virtual world on the other side of the screen and what we still insist on calling "reality," a term that is beginning, in a Facetuned, Deepfaked media landscape made uncanny by AI, to seem almost quaint. For Christopher, this "alien feeling we have yet to assimilate" is a leading indicator of "the merging of technology with the human species." (Of course, our cyborging began with the invention of language, the Ur-technology. With apologies to Bruno Latour, we have never been human.)

At the same time, suggests Christopher, we can also read *Under the Skin* as an attempt to represent the unrepresentable—"this infinite and alien" thing (Glazer), the Nothing. *Post-Self* is very much of its 2020's moment, steeped in the blacker-than-Vantablack pessimism of Eugene Thacker's "Horror of Philosophy" trilogy, the mordant misanthropy of the horror writer Thomas Ligotti (*The Conspiracy Against the Human Race*) and the Nietzschean philosopher E.M. Cioran (*The Trouble With Being Born*). There are, of course, the *de rigeur* references to black-metal theory and the HBO cult hit *True Detective*, whose protagonist "Rust" Cohle (Matthew McConaughey) is quoted by Christopher in an epigraph for his musings on human nature as freakishly unnatural: "I think human consciousness is a tragic misstep in evolution. We became too self-aware. Nature created an aspect of nature separate from itself. We are creatures that should not exist by natural law." Perhaps the "honorable thing for our species to do," Cohle decides, is to "walk hand and hand into extinction" by refusing to reproduce. Embrace the anti-natalism propounded by the moral philosopher David Benatar (*Better Never to Have Been: The Harm of Coming into Existence*). Crank up Godflesh's *Streetcleaner*, which fuses "the monolithic brutality of heavy metal" with pummeling drum-machine rhythms "no human could play," jackhammered into your head by an Alesis HR-16 drum machine. Give yourself over to the cold, inhuman indifference of the cosmos.

Like Thacker, Christopher writes in the lengthening shadow of eco-pocalypse. Climate anxiety hangs over *Post-Self* like a thunderhead. Also like Thacker, he's inclined to believe the only evidence for Homo sapiens' exceptionalism is its self-immolating insistence on making the Earth uninhabitable. They're on the same page as Agent Smith, the malevolent AI in *The Matrix*, who shudders with revulsion at a species that, from his posthuman perspective, is indistinguishable from a virus. "Every mammal on this planet instinctively develops a natural equilibrium with the surrounding environment but you humans do not," he tells a human he's interrogating. "You move to an area and you multiply and multiply until every natural resource is consumed and the only way you can survive is to spread to another area. There is another organism on this planet that follows the same pattern. Do you know what it is? A virus. Human beings are a disease, a cancer of this planet. You're a plague and we are the cure." Both Thacker and Christopher would despair at the May 31, 2025 article in *The Guardian* reporting that, as a result of rural figures worldwide being "vastly underestimated," "there could be billions more people living on Earth than currently thought"; this on a planet already groaning under the weight of 8.2 billion, and whose human population "will peak at about 10.3 billion in the mid-2080s." Misanthropy made easy.

Like Thacker's *In the Dust of This Planet* (a lodestar, for Christopher), *Post-Self* marks the turning point when the Anthropocene becomes the Misanthropocene. As in Thacker's thought, black metal is a philosophical tool for thinking outside—and, crucially, against—the morbid self-regard of the anthropocentric worldview. For Christopher, black metal refashions the angst and anomie that are rites of passage in postwar adolescence into a politics not just of self-loathing but of *species*-loathing. Here, he radicalizes the philosophical school known as Accelerationism: rather than simply flooring the gas pedal on capitalism in order to drive it over a cliff, *Post-Self* harnesses the sociopathic mindset epitomized by the Columbine killers (one of whom Christopher quotes) in the service of a collective embrace of the death drive. "Black metal is about destruction, destroying humanity; destroying one's own self in an orgy of self-loathing and hopelessness," as Black metal band Wolves in the Throne Room have said, quoted in the book's last chapter (bleakly titled "End"). The genre's master metaphor of eternal winter "reveals our sadness and woe as a race. In our hubris, we have rejected the earth and the wisdom of countless generations for the baubles of modernity"—foremost among them our smartphones and social media, fatal distractions at a time when the planetary ecosystem is in a doom spiral.

Then comes the unexpected pivot to the unapologetically misanthropic school of radical environmentalism known as "deep ecology" and the anti-Freudian, anti-anthropocentric insights of "eco-psychology":

> Why are we sad and miserable? Because our modern culture has failed—we are all failures. …The deep woe inside black metal is about fear—that we can never return to the mythic, pastoral world that we crave on a deep subconscious level. Black metal is also about self-loathing, for modernity has transformed us, our minds, bodies, and spirit, into an alien life form; one not suited to life on earth without the mediating forces of technology, culture, and organized religion. We are weak and pitiful in our strength over the earth—in conquering, we have destroyed ourselves.

But there's hope! *Post-Self* dreams, on its next-to-last page, of a post-apocalyptic return to a prelapsarian Eden—no, a paradisal Earth far *better* than the biblical Garden of Earthly Delights because free at last from humanity: a World Without Us, like the one imagined by the science journalist Alan Weisman in his book of the same name, a work of speculative nonfiction.

I'm reminded of Walter Benjamin's recollection, in his essay on Kafka ("Franz Kafka: On the 10th Anniversary of His Death," in *Illuminations*), of a conversation about "the decline of the human race" between the author and his bosom friend Max Brod. "We are nihilistic thoughts, suicidal thoughts that come into God's head," Kafka observes. This reminds Brod of "the Gnostic view of life: God as the evil demiurge, the world as his Fall." Kafka isn't having it: our world, he counters, is only God on a bad day; God in a bad mood. Brod brightens: "Then there is hope outside this manifestation of the world that we know." Kafka smiles—never an auspicious omen. "Oh, plenty of hope," he replies, wryly, "an infinite amount of hope—but not for us."

1

INTRODUCTION

Exit Tragedy

"Living: a body in search of a corpse."

— Eugene Thacker, *Infinite Resignation*[1]

"I think human consciousness is a tragic misstep in evolution. We became too self-aware. Nature created an aspect of nature separate from itself. We are creatures that should not exist by natural law. We are things that labor under the illusion of having a self, an accretion of sensory, experience and feeling, programmed with total assurance that we are each somebody, when in fact everybody is nobody. Maybe the honorable thing for our species to do is deny our programming, stop reproducing, walk hand in hand into extinction, one last midnight, brothers and sisters opting out of a raw deal."

— Rustin Cohle, *True Detective*[2]

We are all perpetually holding ourselves together. Our breath, our blood, our food, our spit, our shit, our thoughts, our attention—all tightly held, all the time. Then at death, we let

---

1 Thacker, Eugene, *Infinite Resignation*, London: Repeater Books, 2018, 128.
2 Pizzolatto, Nic, *True Detective* [Television series], New York: HBO, 2014.

it all out, oozing at once into the earth and gasping at last into the ether.

What if we let it slip before then? What if we were able to let ourselves loose and be as free as we can be? What if we got lost somewhere out there beyond ourselves? If it's all going down, why aren't we trying to push ourselves as far out as we can? If we try to hold ourselves together as we watch our world fall apart, we're holding ourselves back for nothing.

If this sounds like despair, it probably should. The more we realize about our place in the world, the worse that place seems to get. Much has been written about the mainstreaming of pessimism as a philosophy, thanks especially to Rustin Cohle (played by Matthew McConaughey) in season one of Nic Pizzolatto's *True Detective* television series. Echoes of Cohle's morose monologues, themselves echoes of the writings of Thomas Ligotti, Laird Barron, and E. M. Cioran, among others, can be found throughout this book.[3] Gary J. Shipley writes of the show, "The end has already happened, and all Rustin Cohle and Marty Hart [Woody Harrelson] can do is arrange the bodies in a pattern that makes them look less like bodies, more like things that might have existed in bodies, if those bodies hadn't been born human."[4] This resignation is evident

---

3   See Calia, Michael, Writer Nic Pizzolatto on Thomas Ligotti and the Weird Secrets of *True Detective*, *Wall Street Journal*, February 2, 2014: https://www.wsj.com/articles/BL-SEB-79577; Pizzolatto also mentions John Langan, Simon Strantzas, Robert W. Chambers, and Karl Edward Wagner, as well as Edgar Allan Poe and H.P. Lovecraft, among others.

4   Shipley, Gary J., Monster at the End: Pessimism's Locked Rooms and Impossible Crimes, In Edia Connole, Paul J. Ennis & Nicola Masciandaro (Eds.), *True Detection*, Schism, 2014, 2.

not only in this show but many others, a malaise seeping into our minds through our media.

The second season of the show continues the gloom of the first. Though, as Ian Bogost points out, where Cohle got lost in his own head, the characters in season two get lost out in the world.[5] The physician and psychoanalyst Dr. John C. Lilly distinguished between what he called "insanity" and "outsanity." Insanity is "your life inside yourself." Outsanity is the chaos of the world, the cruelty of other people.[6] Dr. Lilly used isolation tanks and psychedelics to explore his mind, leaving his body behind. Sometimes we get lost in our heads. Sometimes we get lost in the world.

As the Earth sustains less and less life, and the life that is left is susceptible to more and more hostile viruses and disease, our physical forms are vulnerable. Growing up under the shadow of the cold war, the end seemed far away, like a mushroom cloud in the distance. The apocalyptic rhetoric of Y2K, the direct attacks of 9/11, and the Mayan calendar collapse of 2012 all brought eschatology ever closer, to mindsets and media outlets everywhere. Given the hostility of the global climate and the polarity of the political climate, as well as the increasingly frequent mass shootings, it now feels like the end is lurking right outside the door, a killer with a knife at the

---

5 Bogost tweeted on Tuesday, August 11, 2015: "By contrast, S2 was pure collapse. Nothing mattered or had meaningful effect. Rust got lost in his head. Ray, Frank, Ani: in the world."

6 See Brown, David Jay, From Here to Alterity and Beyond with John C. Lilly. In David Jay Brown & Rebecca McClen Novick (Eds.), *Mavericks of the Mind: Conversations for the New Millennium.* Berkeley, CA: The Crossing Press, 1993, 206.

ready. If we are to protect ourselves, we must move beyond our selves.

One of the many methods used in futures studies is called environmental scanning. "All futurists do environmental scanning," write Theodore J. Gordon and Jerome C. Glenn, "some are more organized and systematic, all try to distinguish among what is constant, what changes, and what constantly changes."[7] The process, which includes several distant early warning techniques, from expert panels, literature reviews, internet searches, and conference monitoring, helps inform the pursuits of issues management and strategic planning. According to William Renfro, President of the Issues Management Association, issues management consists of four stages: identifying potential future issues, researching the background and potential impacts of these issues, evaluating issues competing for a corporation or nation's operations, and developing appropriate strategies for these operations.[8]

Science fiction stories and horror movies are other places we look to "see" the future. Simulations and speculations are much more fun and much safer than the real things. Spaceships, AI, robots, cyberspace—these all exist in some form in the real world, but the widespread perception of these contrivances comes from fiction. "In the context of SF," Adam Roberts writes, "this reification works most potently on the interconnected levels of representation of technology and the

---

7   Glenn, Jerome C. & Gordon, Theodore J., *Futures Research Methodology, V2.0*. Washington, DC: AC/UNU Millennium Project, 2003, 3.

8   Renfro, William L., *Issues Management in Strategic Planning*. Westport, CT: Quorum Books, 1993, 67.

technologies of reproduction."[9] At varying levels, we look to science fiction and horror to show us the potential directions technology is going and the ways it will affect our lives. These speculative trajectories show us what's possible, even if it's just by showing us what's not.

The art critic Harold Rosenberg argued that the culture of any society is the debris of past cultures, that any current culture is the fallout of the former, more so than a cohesive system itself.[10] When we describe something as ahead of its time, sometimes that means it took a long time to find an audience, but it could be that it was predicting a possible future. In what follows, we will explore scenarios that may not include living on this planet and some that may not include living at all. In order to explore the space after and beyond ourselves, we will employ ideas and artifacts from heavy metal music to science fiction and horror films: the dark debris of recent systems, the prescient, predictive, and prophetic pieces of the past. One possible escape is found in mechanized sound, starting with the heaviest metal of England.

Justin K. Broadrick's best-known band, Godflesh, emerged in the late 1980s from the cold concrete of Birmingham, the same oppressive environment that spawned metal pioneers Black Sabbath and Judas Priest. Godflesh's first full-length record, *Streetcleaner*, provides an

---

9   Adam Roberts, *Science Fiction: The New Critical Idiom* (New York: Routledge, 2006), 113. Roberts adds, "Science as simulation is the reason why fictional science, or 'SF', is so much more fun to watch than real science...".

10 See Victor Turner, *Dramas, Fields, and Metaphors: Symbolic Action in Human Society* (Ithaca, NY: Cornell University Press, 1974), 14.

apocalyptic soundtrack to the world from which it came. *Streetcleaner* plods along at the pace of some giant factory, guitars and bass pummeling to the sound of machines. The overall sound is simply crushing. With the creeping nihilism of nine tons of radioactive sludge, Godflesh grinds and growls through the flaws and floes of humanity. Chapter One establishes the sound of the end and launches us into the remaining themes of this book. Like Godflesh's music, this book is about the space beyond the bounds of the human body and the end of life itself.

Though the name "Godflesh" carries many connotations, one reading is that the body is all-powerful, a true master, no matter the host. "The social body constrains the way the physical body is perceived," wrote the anthropologist Mary Douglas.

The physical experience of the body, always modified by the social categories through which it is known, sustains a particular view of society. There is a continual exchange of meanings between the two kinds of bodily experience so that each reinforces the categories of the other. As a result of this interaction the body itself is a highly restricted medium of expression.[11]

Chapter Two delves into such definitions of the body, seeking a broad view, with a watchful eye for a way around these restrictions. Possible escape routes from our corporeal

---

11 Mary Douglas, *Natural Symbols: Explorations in Cosmology* (London: Barrie & Rockliff, 1970), 65; see also Mary Douglas, *Implicit Meanings: Essays in Anthropology* (London: Routledge & Kegan Paul, 1975).

constraints include machines, rapture, drugs, and death. *Post-Self* includes a chapter on each, concluding with a look at the end of our existence, a glimpse of a future without us.

Turbulent Bloodlines

As cyberculture became culture at large, the body anxieties of the original cyberpunks slowly seeped into the everyday. Often viewed as a threat to human livelihood, mechanization promises freedom from our frail bodies. Some imagine a very deliberate merging, postulating an uploading of human consciousness into the contrivances themselves. If we can build a better body and inhabit it instead of this one, why not? From the exosomatic augmentation of automobiles to the command-and-control of computers, chapter Three explores the marriage of the human and the machine.

If we can't live here, perhaps there's somewhere else out there or some other form we might take. Maybe we'll get beamed up and away, saved from our own destruction by angels or aliens. "The shedding of our borrowed human bodies may be required in order to take up our new bodies belonging to the next world," read a Heaven's Gate poster from 1994. "If you want to leave with us, you must be willing to lose everything of this world in order to have life in the next. Cling to this world and you'll surely die."[12] In chapter Four, we rise with the fallen and take flight with the chosen.

The cover image of Godflesh's debut album, *Streetcleaner*, is a shot from Ken Russell's 1980 movie *Altered States*. The film follows a scientist attempting to escape his body through his mind, using sensory-deprivation tanks and hallucinogens. It

---

12 See *The Shedding of Our Borrowed Human Bodies*, Heaven's Gate, 1994, https://heavensgate.com/book/611.htm.

closely parallels the early work of sensory-deprivation and dolphin intelligence researcher Dr. John C. Lilly. Exploring the extremes of neurophysiology, biophysics, and electronics, Lilly experimented on himself with isolation tanks and ketamine. In Chapter Five, we take a dose and blast off into inner space.

If life is not an option, then we can escape in death. Serial killers, school shooters, mass murderers, suicide bombers, terrorists, world leaders—if the flesh is their god, they are devoted to destroying it. The last resort of escape from the human body is to snuff out the consciousness inside. Eugene Thacker writes,

> There are times when the stupidity of our species is so suffocating that even extinction will not suffice. Then I understand, if only briefly, the other motive for suicide: the need—the desperate need—to be rid of other people.[13]

So, finally, we're all doomed anyway. Wiping us from this world would relieve all of the tensions of the flesh and bring the ultimate, final brutality. Ghost hunting in a world spent spinning, Chapter Seven reads humanity its last rites and hangs around after we're gone, spectral spectators, as if we were able to fulfill the lifelong dream of attending our own funeral.[14]

---

13 Eugene Thacker, *Infinite Resignation* (London: Repeater Books, 2018), 183.

14 See David Leo Rice, "The Overlook Hotel," *The Believer*, October 31, 2017, https://believermag.com/logger/overlook/.

Let us let go and light out for parts known and unknown, within and without. Let's escape our bodies, wandering and lost. If the only way out is through, then we're each already on our way.

2

GODFLESH

Compound Worlds

"Life on earth never settled down to do anything very good. Science ran too far ahead of us too quickly, and the people got lost in a mechanical wilderness, like children making over pretty things, gadgets, helicopters, rockets; emphasizing the wrong items, emphasizing machines instead of how to run the machines. Wars got bigger and bigger and finally killed Earth."

— from Ray Bradbury's *The Martian Chronicles*[1]

"Sometimes I can sit and think about world peace, and sometimes I think I can kill everybody in the world."

— Cary Stayner[2]

"I hope that when the world comes to an end, I can breathe a sigh of relief because there will be so much to look forward to."

— Donnie Darko[3]

---

1   Ray Bradbury, *The Martian Chronicles* (New York: Doubleday, 1950), 180.

2   Quoted in Linda Hayes (writer) and Lisa Quijano Wolfinger (director), *Wild Crime*: "Season 2: Murder in Yosemite" (Los Angeles: Hulu, October 25, 2022).

3   Richard Kelly (writer and director), *Donnie Darko* [motion picture] (Los Angeles: Newmarket, 2001).

"It's just a matter of time, for me, before our ultimate extinction, and I can't say we don't deserve it."[4] This quotation from Justin K. Broadrick sums up his motivation as an artist. His prolific career involving countless bands and projects spans over three decades. But it also says a lot about what many would call his most important band and their most important record. That band is Godflesh, and that record is *Streetcleaner*. "I don't have a very optimistic view of humanity," Broadrick said in the early 1990s, not long after *Streetcleaner* had been unleashed on the world. "Eighty percent of it is shit, and as a whole, mankind is very weak and without any kind of purpose. Once in a while, people need to be crushed emotionally and intellectually to be reminded of reality. That's the basic purpose of our music..."[5] Rebelling against their backgrounds and the very metal scene that spawned them, Broadrick says, "with Godflesh we were like, fuck everyone. And that was obviously cultivated even further to make an album like *Streetcleaner*."[6]

In the late 1980s, metal was fast and heavy. The underground was ruled and regulated by thrash, death metal, and grindcore, each with its own set of stringent rules and rabid fans. Today's wildly popular black metal was still in its infancy. Godflesh's debut was sluggish in comparison, and they used a drum machine instead of a live drummer, anathema in the

---

4   Quoted in Luke Turner, "Greymachine: Justin Broadrick and Aaron Turner United," *The Quietus*, November 18, 2009, https://thequietus.com/interviews/greymachine-justin-broadrick-and-aaron-turner-united/.

5   Quoted in René Walczak, "Godflesh: Strength Through Purity," *Propaganda* no. 19, Fall 1992, 40–41.

6   Quoted in Anthony Bartkewicz, "Vision: Escape: Justin Broadrick," *Decibel Magazine*, March 2007, 71.

stodgy metal underground. "For at least the first year that we played," Broadrick remembers, "there were people chanting, 'Where's the drummer?' or 'You're too fucking slow!'"[7] Their initial reception was not promising, but as Broadrick put it at the time, "It's got a sound, and it's unique. And it's fucking heavy."[8]

In sound and theme, Godflesh's *Streetcleaner* struggles with the limits of human abilities. After leaving his previous hardcore and grindcore bands behind, Broadrick had a vision for a new sound. As a huge hip-hop fan, he wanted to infuse and abuse the monolithic brutality of heavy metal with maniacal, neck-breaking beats no human could play. He enlisted the help of a drum machine, an Alesis HR-16, layering drum sounds into impossibly pummeling rhythms, rhythms no human drummer could maintain. It's the cruelty of all times, crushed together by a post-industrial machine. *Streetcleaner* is a genre-defying and a genre-defining record. In fact, the reunited Godflesh performed the record in its entirety at Holland's Roadburn Festival in 2011, illustrating its lasting influence. "It is an angsty record written by a couple of teenagers," he said of the performance, "and it still resonates now. In fact, even more so, to some extent."[9]

"Godflesh is totally borne from those first twenty-four years of my life that I spent in Birmingham," Broadrick

---

7   Ibid.

8   Quoted in Albert Mudrian, "Just Words from the Editor," *Decibel Magazine*, March 2007, 8.

9   Quoted in J.J. Koczan, "Jesu Interview: Justin Broadrick Confirms New Godflesh Studio Album, Discusses Jesu's Latest, Imperfection, Self-Indulgence, Roadburn, and Much More," *The Obelisk*, May 6, 2011, http://theobelisk.net/obelisk/2011/05/06/jesuinterview/.

remembers.[10] The bleak, industrial environs of Birmingham gave birth to other dark, canonically heavy outfits like Black Sabbath and Judas Priest. The oppression of being "amongst crowds of people, being surrounded by concrete," as he puts it, shaped who Broadrick is, and the way he expresses it. "I don't think Godflesh would have existed if I'd come from another environment. It's absolutely a reflection of the environment that I grew up in."[11] Summing it up succinctly, J.J. Anselmi, author of *Doomed to Fail*, writes,

> Black Sabbath and Napalm Death reflect the negativity of industrial life, but Godflesh recreates the factory and its indifferent thrum. The band's self-titled album forces the brain down conveyer belts and through a maze of steel compactors that never seems to end, mirroring a life of toiling alongside machinery that could so easily grind your bones to dust.[12]

"With Godflesh, we try to aim at something quite off balance, off kilter, a lot different from anyone else,"[13] Broadrick told me in 1996. Since its inception, Godflesh has been Broadrick and Christian "Benny" Green with their drum machine, and

10 Quoted in Roy Christopher, "Godflesh: Uneasy Listening," *Pandemonium!* no. 47, October 1996.

11 Quoted in Dimitri Nasrallah, "Justin Broadrick: Napalm Death – Godflesh – Techno Animal – Jesu – Pale Sketcher," *Exclaim!*, September 2010, https://exclaim.ca/music/article/justin_broadrick-napalm_death-godflesh-techno_animal-jesu-pale_sketcher.

12 J.J. Anselmi, *Doomed to Fail: The Incredibly Loud History of Doom, Sludge, and Post Metal* (Los Angeles: Rare Bird Books, 2020), 213.

13 Quoted in Christopher, "Godflesh: Uneasy Listening."

A couple of teenagers: Benny Green and Justin K. Broadrick are Godflesh

as strange as it may seem for a band as heavy as Godflesh is, hip-hop has been an obvious element in their overall sound. "I think hip-hop is more important than any sort of rock music," states Broadrick matter-of-factly. "Most of the beats are fatter and heavier than your average rock n' roll riff."[14] One of the major sonic tenets of Godflesh is that under the monolithic basslines and ear-searing guitar riffs lie hip-hop's

---

14 Quoted in Roy Christopher, "Godflesh: Heads Ain't Ready," *SLAP Skateboard Magazine*, December 1997.

most brutal breakbeats. Not realizing what a total hip-hop head Justin is, people tend to miss the low-key references to the genre in Godflesh's music. Broadrick describes the collision and collusion of genres inherent in Godflesh's sound:

> I guess one of the things about metal is that it's really stigmatised, even with myself in Godflesh, when we first became somewhat popular, I was very eager at that time to distance myself from metal, and I think that's because at the time there was very little like Godflesh. The most popular metal when Godflesh became popular in 1989/90 was the back-end of the hair metal thing, and Godflesh played with a lot of bands, a lot of tours in America like that, and I became quite repulsed by the whole circus of heavy metal. But, essentially, I've always been excited by what's central to heavy metal, which is the sound, the texture of heavy metal. That was it, for me.[15]

To wit, the beat on the song "Christbait Rising" from *Streetcleaner* was Broadrick's attempt to copy the rhythm break from 1988's "Microphone Fiend" by Eric B. and Rakim. "We have our own bastardized idea of what we can do hip-hop-wise," he tells me. "It comes out even more perverted this way."[16]

In the early 1980s, photocopied fanzines and demo tapes were heavily circulating through underground networks via

---

15 Quoted in Jonathan Horsley, "Justin Broadrick Interview: Godflesh, Growing Up and Anarcho-Punk," *Decibel Magazine*, October 7, 2011, http://www.decibelmagazine.com/featured/justin-broadrick-interview-godflesh-growing-up-and-anarcho-punk/.

16 Quoted in Christopher, "Heads Ain't Ready."

the postal service. Broadrick's interest in extreme music and in finding like-minded individuals naturally landed him in the middle of this subculture. He started his first band, Final, and recorded many cassettes. Through these exchanges, he joined a band called Fall of Because. Benny Green, Paul Neville, and Diarmuid Dalton—all of whom Broadrick still works with in different projects—made up the rest of the band. Broadrick joined them on drums, replacing their drum machine. Fall of Because's one recorded demo, which was compiled with live clips and released as the record *Life is Easy* in 1999, hints at the cold nihilism that would become Godflesh's signature sound.

Broadrick had two more short stops before forming Godflesh proper: He played guitar on the first side of *Scum* (1986), the first record by grindcore pioneers Napalm Death, and drums for the down-tuned, sludgy, metal band Head of David. "Head of David already had an album out," Broadrick explains.

They were the only people I knew who had fans and actually had a record in the shops. It wasn't just opportunistic for me, that first Head of David album I actually adored. I thought it was fucking amazing. With Napalm Death, we played with them a few times, and they were absolutely stunning. When their drummer left, they saw me drum with Fall of Because and invited me to join.[17]

His exit from Head of David was the real beginning of Godflesh "They wanted to lose a lot of the noise and the qualities that had attracted me to that band," he says. "So, when

---

17 Quoted in Nasrallah, "Justin Broadrick."

they kicked me out of the band, I thought, right, I want to do something that takes the basic premise of where I wanted to go with Head of David, low-tune everything, make it brutal,"[18] to take it "to the gutter, make it more machine-like"[19] In the meantime, Fall of Because had broken up, leaving Benny Green free to join Broadrick's new project.

> Godflesh really became my vision, and Ben Green was really into the same type of stuff[...] and we already had our songs from Fall of Because so we began with those[...] I was really influenced by people using drum machines, most notably some of the hip-hop at the time: Public Enemy, Eric B & Rakim. When I first heard some of those records, I was astonished at the brutality of their drum machines, and I really was excited by that sound. I really wanted something inhuman sounding and beyond human capability. And I was already a drummer, so I knew what beats I wanted to hear. I wanted to hear them in the most disgusting, heavy fashion going.[20]

Their self-titled debut EP on Swordfish Records made the promises that 1989's *Streetcleaner* finally delivered on: songs awash in wailing, scraping guitars, dirge-like, lumbering bass lines, brutal, machine-driven beats, and Broadrick's anguished vocals. It was visceral and like nothing else at the time.

---

18 Ibid.
19 Quoted in Bartkewitcz, "Vision: Escape."
20 Quoted in Nasrallah, "Justin Broadrick."

Primal promises: the first cassette. Silent Scream Records, 1990

The second wave of industrial music, a beat-driven and mechanistic subgenre that found its roots in Throbbing Gristle, Einstürzende Neubauten, and Lou Reed's *Metal Machine Music*, was in full swing. Though no one else was mixing metal with machines quite like Godflesh, fueled by the popularity of Ministry, Skinny Puppy, Nine Inch Nails, and the output of Chicago's WaxTrax Records, the movement gave audiences a cultural reference point and made *Streetcleaner* an underground hit for Godflesh and their label Earache Records. It wasn't long before major labels came courting.

Everyone from innovative rappers and producers like El-P of Run the Jewels to more obvious post-metal followers like Isis acknowledge the record's prescience. "At the time when Isis started," singer and guitarist Aaron Turner says, there weren't a lot of other bands exploring that territory; Godflesh were one of the few founding fathers of that sound. They were taking influences from a number of different places and didn't really fit in anywhere."

Isis covered the title track from *Streetcleaner* as homage to its influence on them. "Justin has been ahead of most musicians," attests producer Alap Momin, who used to make noisy tracks for the experimental hip-hop group Dälek,

reinventing genres from grindcore to hip-hop to drum and bass and more for almost twenty-five years. It's pretty insane when someone can pull that off once, but to do it repeatedly in a variety of genres is really ridiculous.

Burton C. Bell of industrial metal band Fear Factory says, "*Streetcleaner* is a fantastically produced and written record; every song is an opus."

"I remember being stunned when I heard that first Korn album," Broadrick said in 2007,

because there's so much Godflesh in that, but used in this commercial way. It was weird. Like, wow, I guess it had to happen at some point; somebody had to take these sorts of sounds and make them digestible.[21]

The full reach of *Streetcleaner*'s influence is difficult to gauge, but it's safe to say that much of what is considered metal in the twenty-first century wouldn't exist without it. Godflesh has always pushed limits in one direction or another.

---

21 Quoted in Bartkewitcz, "Vision: Escape."

Streetcleaner is the germinal industrial-metal hybrid sound that bands all over the world are still trying to recreate, but Godflesh continued innovating. Since officially disbanding Godflesh in 2002, Broadrick has been busy with a band called Jesu, whom he named after the last song on the last Godflesh record, *Hymns* (2001), indicating a continuation of sorts of their spirit if not sound, and his original musical outlet Final, among other various remixes and collaborations. With the reuniting of Godflesh in 2010, Broadrick admits that he finds himself at home in the band. "I think Godflesh is still presenting exactly what I grew up with and exactly what runs through my blood," he said in 2011.

> It's really important that that sense of expression is back in my life. I think I'd lost it through Jesu. But really, it's not just some re-visitation for me, it really feels like I've gone back to what I am in a way.[22]

"*Streetcleaner* was mostly culled from my teenage years," Justin Broadrick tells me more recently,

> so there's a lot of the pain of transitioning from a child to a teenager, and my inability to come to terms with being an adult, and what the adult world brings: the pain of love, the pain of responsibility, etc.

The noisy machine that cleans pavement notwithstanding, the connotations of the name *Streetcleaner* are numerous, and Broadrick has referenced many of them over the years. "I

---

22 Ibid.

change my angle on it often," he says, "chiefly due to 'maturing.'"[23] It's also street slang for an Uzi submachine gun.

"I found it terrifying but also ambiguous and as a consequence very powerful," Broadrick tells me.

> I wanted to revel in the fear of almost everything I experienced as a kid, grasp it, and attempt to become empowered by it, hence making a bloated, filthy, primitive punk-like expression of the term.[24]

As we unpack the themes evident in Godflesh's music in what follows, the connotations and coincidences pile up pretty quickly.

---

23 Email with the author, February 16, 2021.
24 Ibid.

3

BODY

The Root of All People

"I wish I could peel away your humid, human skin
And attach you to me, parasitically."

— Milemarker, "Insect Incest"[1]

"The body, like most things, is a tool. The body's morality depends
on its user. The body's morality is determined by the types and
amounts of consumption it participates in. The body is a filter.
The body is a filter for language. The body is a filter for reality,
which it distills into image. The body filters image. The body is an
image. The body is image."

— from Elle Nash's *Nudes*[2]

"The heart is a rotten root twining
Through soil feasting on droplets."

— George L. Clarke, *Westlake*[3]

---

1   Milemarker, "Insect Incest," on *Sex Jams* [7" single] (New Gretna: Bloodlink Records, 1999).
2   Elle Nash, *Nudes* (Ann Arbor: Short Flight/Long Drive Books, 2020), 148.
3   George L. Clarke, *Westlake and Selected Writings* (Los Angeles: Sargent House, 2017), n.p.

It's not like it looks on TV. You never see the open torso of a body heaving and sucking after a bullet, a piece of shrapnel, or a chunk of flying concrete has ripped right through it. The worst part is the smell: somewhere between bad breath and warm shit. And it's inescapable. If the blood and guts get to be too much, you can look away. You can't get way from the smell.

Bodies are gross. Getting out of them remains one of the most pervasive and persistent human fantasies. Fragile and frail, they fail us. They suffer injuries. They decay. About his music in 2023, Justin Broadrick says, "I want to immerse myself so much it that I don't feel like this shitty human being anymore. I'm not happy in this skin. A lot of my lyrics are wishing for nullification, wishing for an end."[4] From feeling the limits of this sluggish shell to seeing it as a prison cell, everyone is looking for a way out.

Remove This Shell

Regularly referencing the limits of humanity in general and of the human body specifically, the lyrics on Godflesh's *Streetcleaner* include laconic lines like, "you breed, like rats," "bleed dry mankind," "remove this shell," "life / Our life / My life / Is expendable," "There has to be someone killed," "hell / Is where I lie / Now take the power / When we all die / We all die," and "the world shall shed / A tiny tear."[5] Death and extinction appear throughout. It might sound like typical heavy metal fare, but Broadrick bristles at the connotation.

---

4   Quoted in Daniel Lake, "Long May I Dream These Nightmares," *Decibel Magazine*, July 2023, 56.

5   Godflesh, *Streetcleaner* [LP] (London: Earache Records, 1989).

"I've always hated metal," he tells me.

I've just used and abused it. I think people like to think that before we made *Streetcleaner* that we were some long-hair band who'd just discovered industrial music when that's not the case at all. The first music I was into was punk rock. It's so hard to convey these ideas to these people. They always come to me with how metal should go back to what it was in the eighties, and I'm like, "Bloody hell!" I've always found metal rather conservative.[6]

Godflesh has not only always rebelled against the strict confines of genre distinctions, but they never really fit them anyway. *Streetcleaner* grinds and growls like a flailing, failing factory: claustrophobic, misanthropic, foreboding, and forbidding yet dead deliberate in every aspect. "This was the antithesis of the old archaic image of cartoon, all conquering, always male, metal," Broadrick says in 2022.

And I've always felt the absolute opposite. If I want to hurt anyone, it's myself, for a start. And I feel like if it's the enemy of anything, Godflesh was always just the enemy of ignorance in all its forms.[7]

---

6   Quoted in Roy Christopher, "Heads Ain't Ready."
7   Quoted in Antonio Poscic, "Out Demons Out," *The Wire*, April 2022, 30.

Faces of the 'Flesh: Justin Broadrick and Benny Green

Justin Broadrick was born on August 15, 1969 in Birmingham, an "unpleasant" area that he describes as "the Detroit of England."[8] His first few years were spent on an actual hippie commune. Then he, his mom, and stepfather—his biological father was a heroin addict whom he didn't see until he was 15 years old—moved into a council estate, the public housing projects of England. By the age of 12, Broadrick found punk rock like Crass, industrial bands like Throbbing Gristle and Whitehouse, and Krautrock like Can, as well as Brian Eno's early ambient work, all of which would inform his own musical output. He started messing around with some of his stepfather's music gear and taught himself guitar. "[W]hen I began to play guitar," he explains,

> I mastered one bar chord and realized that I could play any Crass song I wanted. That was pretty satisfying in itself.

---

8   Quoted in Nasrallah, "Justin Broadrick."

"Music" was like a dirty word when I went to school in 1978. Everyone was just into football hooliganism. But at home, I was absolutely inspired at a very young age to act in my environment, both in the form of music and, to some extent, against the oppressive environment I was in.[9]

Finding oneself trapped in a body can be a traumatic experience. When that body is walled-in by a city with cement and a family fraught with addiction, escape is high priority. When that body is left all alone, isolated from all other bodies, escape is high priority.

In the meantime, we put a lot on them. Bodies provide us with the illusion of permanence. For some of us, the body is a canvas, here to display the trials and traumas of the mind. We tattoo them with the symbols and sigils of our life's stories, its highs and lows that we don't want to forget. Our bodies display the scars of jumps and falls, attempts and fails. For others, the body is merely a vessel to carry them through this life, a physical manifestation of a time on this planet. Either way, we adorn them, embellish them, cover them, uncover them, care for them, curse them, protect them, mutilate them, use them, abuse them, augment them, extend them.

Boundary Trouble

Once declaring that an individual is a "montage of loosely assembled parts," and furthermore that when "you are on the phone or on the air you have no body,"[10] Marshall McLuhan's brand of media theory

---

9 Ibid.

10 Marshall McLuhan, *The Gutenberg Galaxy: The Making of Typographic Man* (Toronto: University of Toronto Press, 1962), xxix.

dismembered the body. The music and media we make, as well as the machines we use to make them are all extensions of ourselves in McLuhan's terms, but they're also prosthetics, amputating parts of ourselves as they extend them, turning us into cyborgs. Judith Butler reassembles the body as "culturally intelligible";[11] that is, as one that is recognized by the members of its society, what Sandy Stone calls the "legible body."[12] On the phone, on the air, or online, you are "read" as a member. Stone also postulates the "illegible body" that exists "quantumlike in multiple states":

> their social system includes other people, quasi people or delegated agencies that represent specific individuals, and quasi agents that represent "intelligent" machines, clusters of people, or both.[13]

This discourse doesn't just fragment the body into gendered, sexualized, augmented, and virtual codes and constructs, but also addresses the fact that concerns about the body haven't been marginalized by technological evolution as largely predicted. Just as telecommuting de-emphasizes place in that we can work from anywhere, it reemphasizes it in that where we are

---

11 Judith Butler, *Gender Trouble: Feminism and the Subversion of Identity* (New York: Routledge, 1990), 167.

12 Allucquère Rosanne (Sandy) Stone, "Will the Real Body Please Stand Up?," in *Reading Digital Culture*, ed. David Trend (Malden: Blackwell, 2001), 195.

13 Ibid., 196.

matters more. Not having a body or having a techno-logically mediated one now matters in a different way.

Even from a steadfastly feminist stance, we tend to focus on the narratives and discourses surrounding issues of the body more so than their material systems and conditions. As Donna Haraway, the author of "The Cyborg Manifesto," puts it, "the cyborg is a kind of disassembled and reassembled, postmodern collective and personal self."[14] N. Katherine Hayles adds that cyborgs are "simultaneously entities and metaphors, living beings, and narrative constructions."[15] In such a muddled milieu, the power lies in the control of these analogies and their boundaries. Without the philo-sophical consideration and creative expression that art provides us, trying to conceive of a self beyond the body is pointless.

Another term for the feminist in Haraway's work is the posthuman, and the philosopher Rosi Braidotti pushes the analogies and boundaries of the body past postmodernity in her 2013 book, *The Posthuman.* Cybernetics defined humans as "information-process-ing systems whose boundaries are determined by the flow of information."[16] Braidotti pays special attention to these flows, building from three areas of thought: moral

---

14 Donna J. Haraway, *Simians, Cyborgs, and Women: The Reinvention of Nature* (New York: Routledge, 1990), 163.

15 N. Katherine Hayles, *How We Became Posthuman: Virtual Bodies in Cybernetics, Literature, and Informatics* (Chicago: University of Chicago Press, 1999), 114.

16 Ibid., 114. Hayles adds, "when system boundaries are defined by infor-mation flows and feedback loops rather than epidermal surfaces, the

philosophy, science and technology, and anti-humanist philosophies of subjectivity. Paul Virilio extended the term "cyberspace" to its imaginary, original form "cybernetic space-time,"[17] which evokes the ultimate mechanical prosthesis of the mind, a planet-spanning, command-control system to end all such systems. Even now, a globalized network culture decentralizes the humanist subject's stability in space and time. The upending of anthropocentrism upsets the hierarchy of the species, and the technological mediation of the human subject disrupts our ideas about bodily norms.

The body's boundaries are permeable. Not so permanent after all, in the long tail of gender, the body's own physical signifiers are less important than how we feel within them. Moving beyond the body as we know it means subverting any extant grand narrative or theory of the embodied human and any attempt at a new one. It means rejecting the demonization of science and technology. It means embracing the non-linearity of our posthuman times, the further fragmentation of our selves, and the permeability of our bodily

---

subject becomes a system to be assembled and disassembled rather than an entity whose organic wholeness can be assumed" (160).

17 Paul Virilio, *The Art of the Motor* (Minneapolis: University of Minnesota Press, 1995), 140. Bradotti writes, "in the perspective of French Post-structuralism, the human organic mass, the body, is the first manufacturer of technology in that it seeks for organic extension of itself first through tools, weapons, and artifacts, then through language, the ultimate prosthesis." Rosi Braidotti, *Nomadic Subjects: Embodiment and Sexual Difference in Contemporary Feminist Theory* (New York: Columbia University Press, 1994), 44.

boundaries and definitions. Haraway writes, "it means both building and destroying machines, identities, relationships."[18] It means rethinking the lines we've drawn through the ones we've crossed.[19]

Any attempt to escape the body only reifies its limits. Every augmentation brings its own detriment. Every route out has its own pitfalls.[20]

This is the Voice[21]

The tagline to the 2009 movie *Moon* reads, "250,000 miles from home, the hardest thing to face... is yourself." *Moon* tells the story of astronaut Sam Bell, who on his last two weeks of a three-year solitary contract harvesting Helium 3 from the far side of the Moon, out of sight of Earth. During his last two weeks of his lunar stay, the daily routine of his mission starts to devolve into madness and second-guessing. Sam is haunted by hallucinations of a teenage girl and an older man. Overwhelmed, he chants, "Two more weeks, two more weeks" like a mantra.

Even though his existence on the Moon is largely attended to by communication media and technology, Sam can't escape himself. He is alone aside from his

---

18 Donna J. Haraway, *Simians, Cyborgs, and Women*, 181.

19 See Brian Rotman, *Becoming Beside Ourselves: The Alphabet, Ghosts, and Distributed Human Being* (Durham: Duke University Press, 2008).

20 As Shipley puts it, "it is for this reason that the way out is always nothing, always negative, always elusive and void: God, reality, death, ourselves." Gary J. Shipley, *Stratagem of the Corpse: Dying with Baudrillard, a Study of Sickness and Simulacra* (London: Anthem Press, 2020), 34.

21 Agent Orange, *This is the Voice* [LP] (Los Angeles: Enigma Records, 1986).

computerized companion, and the messages he sends to and receives from earth are prerecorded, unbeknownst to him. Even in its celestial setting, *Moon* is more concerned with inner space than outer space. Writer and director Duncan Jones wrote the role of Sam Bell specifically for Sam Rockwell, and his having the same first name is no accident. Jones explains, "one of the reasons why I left the name Sam is I wanted [Rockwell] to have that feeling of it being a little uncomfortable, that he's having to face himself, because in the story, that's what happens."[22]

Sam I am: Sam Rockwell as Sam Bell in *Moon*, 2009

22 Quoted in Marjorie Baumgarten, "Sitting in a Tin Can, Where Hell Is Still Other People: Director Duncan Jones on his debut film, 'Moon,'" *The Chronicle*, July 10, 2009.

Now, is the fissure caused by the Mother, the Father, or the Other? In *Moon*, there's more than one Sam. Actually, there are more than two Sams. Judith Butler asks, "what if there is an Other who does violence to another Other?"[23] What we think is the original Sam on the Moon eventually encounters two other Sams, and two of them find a store of endless Sams. Aching to resolve his existential identity crisis, the Sam we've followed from the beginning calls his wife on Earth. His daughter, Eve, answers the videophone, and explains that his wife died years before. During their brief conversation, he hears his own voice from off screen. This opens the real fissure. Recognizing the sound of his own voice after a moment of detachment, Sam immediately hangs up. The words spoken from Earth do not matter; only the voice with which they are spoken. Seeing himself in the flesh on the Moon was one kind of encounter. Hearing himself speak from Earth was more than he could take. Butler writes, "we cannot, under contemporary representation, hear the agonized cry or be compelled or commanded by the face."[24] Only the voice can do this. The voice is the presence of the real.

The voice without language is the seat of suffering.[25] Like machine parts pushed past their limits, cogs

---

23 Butler, *Gender Trouble*, 139.

24 Ibid., 150. Steve Connor adds, "the voice may be grasped as the mediation between the phenomenological body and its social and cultural contexts." Steve Connor, *Dumbstruck: A Cultural History of Ventriloquism* (Oxford: Oxford University Press, 2000), 12.

25 Rotman writes, "the affect proper to human speech, which pertains to moods, feelings, passions, attitudes, or emotions it conveys and induces,

stripped bare of their teeth, language lost to pain brings us back to the body. When Sam hears the sound of his own voice on the line to Earth, he is returned to himself. Witness Broadrick's howls or the shrieks and shrills of other metal vocalists. In these extreme musical forms, the voice is employed as another instrument or texture. Mladen Dolar writes, "as soon as it departs from its textual anchorage, the voice becomes senseless and threatening."[26] Moreover, when technology tethers the voice with language through text or some other media, we are aware of the Other and sometimes our own Other. We do not like to realize ourselves as Other. We do not like to realize the humanity of the Other. These realizations are nowhere more present than in the voice. Seeing is one thing. There remains a distance to the visual. Hearing is in your head. Dolar challenges the primacy of the visual by positioning the voice as "the first manifestation of life."[27] That is, before the image of the mirror, before self-recognition via the gaze, it is

---

lies in its tone, a phenomenon determined by the gestures of the voice, those auditory movements of the body within utterance: its hesitations, silences, emphases, sharpness, timbre, musicality, changes of pitch, and other elements of prosody. The alphabet knows nothing of all this. It eliminates tone and any kind of prosody completely: it reduces the voice to words and writes 'what's said' but not the manner of its saying, its delivery, how what's said is said. What, one can ask, would be the features of a 'speaker': and the affect of a 'voice' known only through alphabetic writing?" Rotman, *Becoming Beside Ourselves*, xxxiii.

26 Mladen Dolar, *A Voice and Nothing More* (Cambridge: The MIT Press, 2006), 43.

27 Ibid., 39.

through our voices and our media that we realize that we are, and that we are Other. Dolar adds, "the voice is both the subtlest and most perfidious form of the flesh."[28] The voice of pain or the voice of the Other gets right inside you.

Sound mind, sound body: the body is inescapable, even if only in sound.

---

28 Ibid., 48.

4

MACHINE

Mechanical Reproduction

"Nothing of us will survive. We will be killed not by the gun but by the glad-hand.
We will be destroyed not by the rocket but by the automobile…"
— Ettil in Ray Bradbury's "The Concrete Mixer"[1]

"It is clear that the car crash is seen as a fertilizing rather than a destructive experience, a liberation of sexual and machine libido, mediating the sexuality of those who have died with an erotic intensity impossible in any other form."
— from J.G. Ballard's *Atrocity Exhibition*[2]

"The lost and found are incalculable."
— Fred Moten, *Black and Blur*[3]

I ordered the seven-inch of Jawbox's 1993 single "Motorist" as soon as I knew it was available. The lyrics, even for a Jawbox

---

1   Ray Bradbury, *The Illustrated Man* (New York: Doubleday, 1951), 225.

2   J.G. Ballard, *The Atrocity Exhibition* (London: Jonathan Cape, 1970), 157.

3   Fred Moten, *Black and Blur: Consent Not to Be a Single Being* (Durham: Duke University Press, 2017), xvii.

song, were striking. "Accidental, maybe," ponders J. Robbins, "restraints too frayed to withhold me."[4] Paul Virilio once wrote that whenever we invent a new technology, we also invent a new kind of accident.[5] We might never again invent a technology that is so prone to accidents as we have with the automobile. Hearing Jawbox play that song live again reminded me of the wreckage of artifacts piled up in my head around it.

Over Zach Borocas's lurching beat, Kim Coletta's chugging bass, and his and Bill Barbot's dual, dueling guitar feedback, Robbins yells, "when you examined the wreck, what did you see? Glass everywhere and wheels still spinning free."[6] I remember immediately thinking of the 1973 Ballard novel, *Crash*. In the simplest of terms, *Crash* is about a group of people who fetishize car crashes. Most of them have been in actual accidents, but they also stage their own. They are sexually aroused by the impact as well as the aftermath, the energies and the injuries.

Though I hadn't read it, I figured Robbins had. While back in Chicago during the last night of the band's 2019 summer reunion tour, Robbins told the story on stage at the Metro, something about a car crash witnessed during a previous tour. In the meantime, Robbins tells me that the song is actually about a tragic relationship,

the sort of relationship in which each person is uniquely equipped to push the buttons of the other's unhealthy

---

4   J. Robbins, "Motorist," on *Jackpot Plus* [7" single], recorded by Jawbox (Washington, DC: Dischord Records, 1993).

5   Paul Virilio, "The Museum of Accidents," trans. Chris Turner, *International Journal of Baudrillard Studies* 3, no. 2 (2006).

6   Robbins, "Motorist."

inherited behaviors. The need to rescue and be rescued is in there, the idea of crashing the car on purpose in order either to occasion an opportunity to become the hero of the story, or the powerless victim of a cruel circumstance.[7]

In light of this new information, I've tried to rewire my interpretation of the song. In my head, Jawbox's "Motorist" remains connected to Ballard's *Crash*.

Robbins is a Ballard fan, telling me,

Ballard is such a hero to me, in whose unique voice I recognized a worldview that resonated with me more than any other writer I had encountered at that point, and to whom I owe a considerable debt for helping me take baby steps along the endless path to finding a voice of my own. Both the Jawbox song and Ballard's book signify "a sort of primitive posthumanism."[8]

Compare Robbins' singing:

Cracked gauges carry messages for me. Calls and responses you can't see;[9]

7   Email to the author, March 22, 2025; Robbins adds, "'Motorist' is not about any real-life event. When we played it in Chicago in 2019, Bill [Barbot] tried to get me to tell a story about the song on stage, but I demurred, saying only that it takes place in 'a Chicago of the mind.'"

8   Simon Sellars, "Learning to Live with Aggressionless Cars," *Foreground*, April 15, 2021. https://www.foreground.com.au/transport/learning-to-live-with-aggressionless-cars/.

9   Robbins, "Motorist."

to Ballard's writing:

> *In front of me the instrument panel had been buckled inwards, cracking the clock and speedometer dials. Sitting here in this deformed cabin, filled with dust and damp carpeting, I tried to visualize myself at the moment of collision, the failure of the technical relationship between my own body, the assumptions of the skin, and the engineering structure which supported it;[10]*

or

> *The wounds on my knees and chest were beacons tuned to a series of beckoning transmitters, carrying the signals, unknown to myself, which would unlock this immense stasis and free these drivers for the real destinations set for their vehicles, the paradises of the electric highway.[11]*

This motorized mysticism, the idea that technology enables and endures unintended uses and conjures and communicates unintended messages runs parallel to the cult of the car. Scriptures superimposed on the roads. Messages, transmissions, signals—all performing a discourse of dread, a dialogue of deadly trauma.

"I'm proud of some lines in the song, but it's also a bit of a mess," Robbins concludes.

Like many Jawbox lyrics, it steals as much from *Concrete Island* as it does from *Crash*. And like many Jawbox lyrics,

---

10 J.G. Ballard, *Crash: A Novel* (London: Jonathan Cape, 1973), 68.
11 Ibid., 44.

it's mostly bashed together phrases that suggest a story but are mostly aiming to occasion a shot at catharsis over a painful situation I didn't fully understand.[12]

Not even understanding will save us.

Crash Worship

Automobile-accident numbers are routinely trotted out in comparison to whatever disaster is threatening human lives at the time. Gun violence, viral plagues, and various cancers are all measured at least annually against the deaths we inflict driving these vehicles. As Zadie Smith writes in *The Guardian*, quoting Ballard himself,

> like the characters in *Crash* we are willing participants in what Ballard called 'a pandemic cataclysm that kills hundreds of thousands of people each year and injures millions.' The death-drive, Thanatos, is not what drivers secretly feel, it's what driving explicitly *is*.[13]

In R. Scott Bakker's 2009 novel *Neuropath*, a character says, "In the physics of car accidents, our body is little more than a rubber bag filled with blood. Go fast enough, and it's like throwing water balloons."[14] When we hear the stories and statistics, we might worry for a second, noting those we know who've passed away on the road or been maimed by molded

---

12 Email to the author, March 22, 2025.

13 Zadie Smith, "Sex and Wheels: Zadie Smith on J.G. Ballard's 'Crash,'" *The Guardian*, July 4, 2014, https://www.theguardian.com/books/2014/jul/04/zadie-smith-jg-ballard-crash.

14 R. Scott Bakker, *Neuropath* (New York: Tor, 2009), 263.

metal, but we soon continue our car-enabled commutes unde-
terred, autocide awaiting.[15]

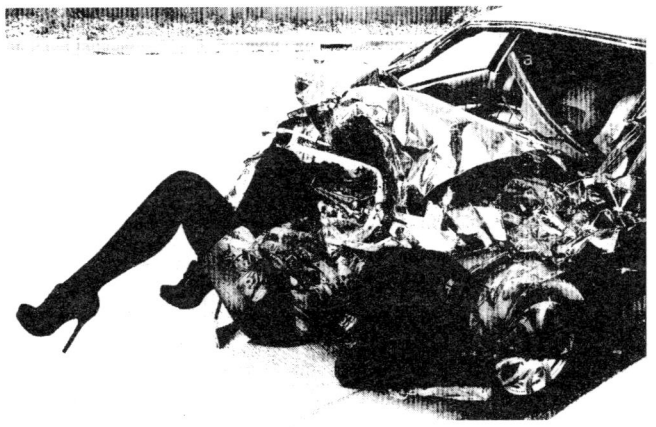

Eros on the Highway. Wreckage by Roy Christopher

Death isn't the only Freudian trope that these stories stir up.
Sex is wound into the car accident as well, both as pornography and as intimacy. "When Ballard called *Crash* the first
'pornographic novel about technology'," Smith continues,
"he referred not only to a certain kind of content but to pornography as an organizing principle."[16] Pornography is itself
a form of media that stimulates the body. We might not enjoy
it or admit that we do, but we all understand it as a concept.
Its meaning is not a mystery. In *Crash*, it acts as a skewed
skeuomorph. As Ballard writes, it is "as if the presence of

---

15 I lifted the word "autocide" from Anthony Smith, *The Body* (New
    York: Walker & Company, 1968), 306.

16 Smith, "Sex and Wheels."

the car mediated an element which alone made sense of the sexual act."[17] And aren't cars always already sexualized? The metaphor is close at hand, as visceral as it is vehicular: pistons and spark plugs, revving and thrusting, hands gripping curves and contours galore.

The jutting juxtaposition of body parts and auto parts and the blending of bodily fluids and engine oils might be more disturbing when thought of as intimacy than as pornography. In Julia Ducournau's *Titane* (2021), the shock of Alexia (played by Agathe Rousselle) having intercourse with automobiles quickly fades. What lingers are the moments when she is simply affectionate toward them, hugging or caressing their cold, metal exteriors. "The real shock of *Crash* is not that people have sex in or near cars," Smith writes, "but that technology has entered into even our most intimate human relations."[18] It's not the violence of the sex act but the intimate presence of technology there that chafes our sensibilities.[19] It's not the sexual appropriation of a mechanical contrivance but the emotional possibility of love that bothers us. "Traditional warnings against the evils of mediation reach an ironic zenith in this portrait of 'the most terrifying casualty of the century: the death of affect,'"[20] Dominic Pettman notes

---

17 Ballard, *Crash*, xii.

18 Smith, "Sex and Wheels."

19 For examples regarding David Cronenberg's 1996 film adaptation, see Martin Barker, Jane Arthors, and Ramaswami Harindranath, *The Crash Controversy: Censorship Campaigns and Film Reception* (London: Wallflower Press, 2001).

20 Dominic Pettman, *After the Orgy: Toward a Politics of Exhaustion* (Albany: SUNY Press, 2002), 80. Pettman is quoting V. Vale and

grimly. With sex and technology crammed together in this context, we can't decide if it's better or worse to care.

No matter how you feel about them, car crashes and sexual encounters force one thing on everyone: exposure. From fender benders to total immobility, no one wants to get caught in the act, caught with their pants down, *in flagrante delicto*. Ballard himself described *Crash* as a forced look in the mirror.[21] "You can see your reflection in the luminescent dash," Daniel Miller sings on The Normal's *Crash*-inspired track, "Warm Leatherette."[22] "Seduced reflection in the chrome," Siouxsie Sioux adds on the Creatures' Ballardian "Miss the Girl."[23] "New way to see what's laid plain in front of me," Robbins wails on "Motorist." "Nothing better than a look at what I shouldn't see."[24] The car accident seen as porn, a form we can't look away from.

No one wants to get caught with their body thrown clear at odd angles, the contents of their car strewn, the whole of

---

Andrea Juno, eds., *RE/Search #8/9: J.G. Ballard* (San Francisco: Re/ Search Publications, 1984).

21 Quoted in Peter Bradshaw, Deyan Sudjic, Dave Simpson, Iain Sinclair, and Mark Lawson, "How J.G. Ballard Cast His Shadow Right Across the Arts," *The Guardian*, April 20, 2009, https://www.theguardian.com/books/2009/apr/20/jg-ballard-film-music-architecture-tv. They themselves quote a sample of Ballard speaking from the Manic Street Preachers song "Mausoleum," on *The Holy Bible* [LP] (New York: Epic Records, 1984).

22 Daniel Miller, "T.V.O.D.," on *Warm Leatherette* [7" single], recorded by The Normal (London: Mute Records, 1978).

23 Siouxsie Sioux and Budgie, "Miss the Girl," on *Feast* [LP], recorded by The Creatures (London: Polydor, 1983).

24 Robbins, "Motorist."

their very lives lying limp on the pavement. Every illicit tryst implies its own exit strategy. On "Motorist," Robbins concludes, "turn your back, just drive on past, because nothing is better than getting out fast."[25]

Look hard and then look away. The fastest car is the getaway.

Uncanny Cartographies

It's been over a decade. A decade without J.G. Ballard. It should be more noticeable. Like filling an empty pool with emptiness, to paraphrase China Miéville.[26] A void of perspective, crumbling and gaping at our heels. Everyone should feel it. It goes without saying, but I'll say it anyway: this is the way, step inside.

His work has been translated to the screen by directors with styles as varied as Steven Spielberg (*Empire of the Sun*, 1987) and David Cronenberg (*Crash*, 1996). He was interviewed by countless talented writers, including Jon Savage, V. Vale, Will Self, Richard Kadrey, John Gray, and Mark Dery.[27] His influence is found in sound from Joy Division, The Jesus and Mary Chain, Sisters of Mercy, K.K. Null, and Gary Numan to Madonna, Radiohead, Trevor Horn, Cadence Weapon, and Danny Brown, as well as the aforementioned Creatures and The Normal. His writing and thinking are broad enough to elude categories and focused enough to remain absolutely singular. His work

---

25 Ibid.

26 China Miéville, "Introduction," in *Miracles of Life: Shanghai to Shepperton, an Autobiography*, by J.G. Ballard (New York: Liveright, 2008), ix–xiv.

27 See, for example, Ballard, *Extreme Metaphors*, passim.

gerrymanders categorical distinctions, defining and defying its own boundaries as it goes. I think of him in the same way I think of Octavia Butler, Ray Bradbury, Thomas Pynchon, Don DeLillo, and Samuel Delany—as giants beyond genre.

"I suppose we are moving into a realm where inner space is no longer just inside our skulls but is in the terrain we see around us in everyday life," Ballard said in 1974;

> we are moving into a world where the elements of fiction are that world—and by fiction I mean anything invented to serve imaginative ends, whether it is invented by an advertising agency, a politician, an airline, or what have you. These elements have now crowded out the old-fashioned elements of reality.[28]

Since then, a lot of mental offloading and cognitive outsourcing has occurred, our inner thoughts texture-mapped onto every surface. In that meantime some of Ballard's children have emerged in mongrel forms and curtained corners of mass media. Think *Wild Palms* or *Jackass* or the ever-blurring lines between reality and show, news and entertainment. "It's not news," Ballard wrote, "it's entertainment news. A documentary on brain surgery is about entertainment brain surgery." Inversely, Ballard collaged and kludged together the sets of his own *Atrocity Exhibition* out of internal organs:

> the nervous systems of the characters have been externalized, as part of the reversal of the interior and exterior

---

28 Quoted in J.G. Ballard, *Extreme Metaphors: Collected Interviews*, eds. Simon Sellars and Dan O'Hara (London: Fourth Estate, 2012), 62.

worlds. Highways, office blocks, faces, and street signs are perceived as if they were elements in a malfunctioning central nervous system.[29]

Having lost his wife to pneumonia in 1964, Ballard began writing the despondently dark stories that would become *The Atrocity Exhibition*. The fully formed dystopia of *Crash* came not long after. Unlike the cyberpunks who followed him, Ballard's views of these near futures weren't as celebratory as they were cautionary: Dangerous Curves Ahead. Slow Down.[30]

Mistaken Algorithms

Ballard's warnings notwithstanding, still we persist. Cinema is our most viable and enduring form of design fiction. More than any other medium, it lets us peer into possible futures projected from the raw materials of the recent past, simulate scenes based on new visions via science and technology,

---

29 Ballard, *The Atrocity Exhibition*, 76.

30 As Ballard wrote in his introduction to *Crash*, "Needless to say, the ultimate role of *Crash* is cautionary, a warning against that brutal, erotic and overlit realm that beckons more and more persuasively to us from the margins of the technological landscape."; Quoted in Pallavi Rao, "J.G. Ballard's (1995) introduction to 'Crash,'" *In a Brown Study*, March 7, 2012: https://uglywords.wordpress. com/2012/03/07/on-j-g-ballards-1995-introduction-to-crash-6-2/; Michel de Certeau once wrote, "Books are only metaphors of the body. But in times of crisis, paper is no longer enough for the law, and it writes itself on the bodies themselves." Ballard often seemed to be crash-testing that idea. Michel de Certeau, *The Practice of Everyday Life* (Berkeley: University of California Press, 1984), 140.

gauge our reactions, and adjust our plans accordingly. These visions are equipment for living in a future heretofore unseen. As the video artist Bill Viola puts it,

> The implied goal of many of our efforts, including technological development, is the eradication of signal-to-noise ratio, which in the end is the ultimate transparent state where there is no perceived difference between the simulation and the reality, between ourselves and the other. We think of two lovers locked in a single ecstatic embrace. We think of futuristic descriptions of direct stimulation to the brain to evoke experiences and memories.[31]

When we think of the future, the images we conjure end up on the screen.

With only one adaptation, director David Cronenberg proved perhaps Ballard's most effective cinematic interpreter. Roger Ebert said of his version of *Crash*, "it's like a porno movie made by a computer: it downloads gigabytes of information about sex, it discovers our love affair with cars, and it combines them in a mistaken algorithm."[32] These visions of intimate machines give both versions of *Crash* a sense of malign prophecy. Before *Crash* in 1996, an adaptation Ballard loved, Cronenberg had already established himself as the preeminent body-horror director with such films as *The Brood* (1979), *Scanners*, (1981), *Videodrome* (1983), *The*

---

31 Bill Viola, *Reasons for Knocking at an Empty House: Writings 1973–1994* (Cambridge: The MIT Press, 1995).

32 Roger Ebert, "'Crash' (1997)," *RogerEbert.com*, March 21, 1997, http://www.rogerebert.com/reviews/crash-1997.

Fly (1986), *Dead Ringers* (1988), and *Naked Lunch.* (1991). Jessica Kiang writes of *Crash*,

> Koteas's Vaughan explains that his project is "the reshaping of the human body through technology," a pretty perfect summation of a recurring theme in the first half of Cronenberg's career, best exemplified by his 1983 masterpiece, *Videodrome*.[33]

In *Videodrome*, CIVIC-TV's satellite dish operator, Harlan (played by Peter Dvorsky) pirates the signal of a plotless show of pure violence called "Videodrome" being beamed from bands in between. In search of unique programming for the station, Max Renn (played by James Woods) authorizes its rebroadcast. Renn soon finds that the footage is not faked and is PR for a socio-political movement weaponizing the signal for mind control. Professor Brian O'Blivion (played by Jack Creley) helped develop the signal to unify the minds of the viewers. *Videodrome* gave him a brain tumor and

---

33 Jessica Kiang, "'Crash': The Wreck of the Century," *The Criterion Collection*, December 1, 2020, https://www.criterion.com/current/posts/7206-crash-the-wreck-of-the-century. She continues, "so, when Vaughan later retracts that statement, calling it 'a crude sci-fi concept that floats on the surface and doesn't threaten anybody,' it's hard not to see Cronenberg slyly denigrating his own back catalog, or at least marking in boldface the end of his ongoing engagement with it. Sure enough, with the exception of a watered-down workout in 1999's *eXistenZ*, *Crash* does represent a move away from the gleefully visceral grotesqueries of his early career, toward the more refined psychological grotesqueries of his twenty-first-century output."

subsequent hallucinations. He sees the resultant state as a higher form of reality. As his daughter explains,

> he saw it as part of the evolution of man as a technological animal. [...] He became convinced that public life on television was more real than private life in the flesh. He wasn't afraid to let his body die.[34]

He tells Max,

> the battle for the mind of North America will be fought in the video arena, the Videodrome. The television screen is the retina of the mind's eye. Therefore, the screen is part of the physical structure of the brain. Therefore, whatever appears on the television screen emerges as raw experience for those who watch it. Therefore, television is reality, and reality is less than television.[35]

It doesn't take long for the reality in this film to devolve into a hallucinatory state itself. As the dialog of the last scene goes,

> to become the new flesh you have to kill the old flesh. Don't be afraid. Don't be afraid to let your body die. [...] Watch. I'll show you how. It's easy. Long live the new flesh. Long live the new flesh.[36]

---

34 David Cronenberg (writer/director), Videodrome [motion picture] (Montreal: Alliance Communications, 1983).

35 Ibid.

36 Ibid.

User Friendly

The media philosopher Matteo Pasquinelli writes,

> Well before the consolidation of mathematics and geometry, ancient civilizations were already great social segmentation machines that marked human bodies and territories with abstractions that have remained and will continue to remain operational for millennia. Also referring to the work of the historian Lewis Mumford, Gilles Deleuze, and Félix Guattari offered a list of these ancient techniques of abstraction and social segmentation: "tattoo, cut, engrave, carve, scarify, mutilate, scratch, start." Numbers were already elements of the "primitive abstract machines" of social segmentation and territorialization that would have brought about human civilization: the first documented census, for example, took place in Mesopotamia around 3800 BC. Logical forms made up of social forms.[37]

Yale University professor Dr. José M.R. Delgado's 1969 book, *Physical Control of the Mind: Toward a Psychocivilized Society*, provides an intriguing precursor to Cronenberg's film. In this book, Delgado outlines the methodology for Cronenberg's fictional conceit. Delgado wrote,

> by means of ESB (electrical stimulation of the brain) it is possible to control a variety of functions—a move-

---

37 Matteo Pasquinelli, "Three Thousand Years of Algorithmic Rituals," *Il Tascabile*, March 15, 2021, https://www.iltascabile.com/scienze/rituali-algoritmici/.

ment, a glandular secretion, or a specific mental manifestation, depending on the chosen target.[38]

While admitting that the brain is protected by layers of bone and membrane, he illustrates how easily it is accessed through the senses, drawing convenient comparisons between garage-door openers and two-way radios, and light waves and optical nerves. Direct brain interfaces through implants have existed since the 1930s when W.R. Hess wired a cat's hypothalamus with electrodes. Hess was able to induce everything from urination and defecation to hunger, thirst, and extreme excitement.

Given the limited viability of such technology during the writing of Delgado's book, he speculates the future of what he calls "stimoceivers," writing,

it is reasonable to speculate that in the near future the stimoceiver may provide the essential link from man to computer to man, with reciprocal feedback between neurons and instruments which represents a new orientation for the medical control of neurophysiological functions.[39]

Though Delgado's stimoceivers are becoming more and more viable, they still require the mind and the machine to adapt to each other.

---

38 José M.R. Delgado, *Physical Control of the Mind: Toward a Psychocivilized Society* (New York: Harper & Row, 1969), 80.

39 Ibid., 91.

Wetware meets hardware: Godflesh's *Selfless*, 1994

The cover of *Selfless*, Godflesh's 1994 record, is a picture of human nerve cells growing on a microchip. It's a picture of what's called neuromorphic computing, a field of artificial intelligence that goes beyond using models of the human brain to physically harness its computing power, either by growing cells on chips or putting chips in brains. In August of 2020, Elon Musk debuted Tesla's Neuralink brain implant, demonstrating the device on three unsuspecting pigs.[40] The

---

40 See Leah Crane, "Elon Musk Demonstrated a Neuralink Brain Implant in a Live Pig," *NewScientist*, August 29, 2020, https://www. newscientist.com/article/2253274-elon-musk-demonstrated-a-neuralink-brain-implant-in-a-live-pig. See also Melissa Heikkilä, "Machines Can Read Your Brain. There's Little That Can Stop Them," *Politico*, August 31, 2021, https://www.politico.eu/article/machines-brain-neurotechnology-neuroscience-privacy-neurorights-protection.

small, coinlike device reads neural activity, and Musk hopes they will eventually write it as well, connecting brains and computers in a completely new way, mirroring neurons and computer chips. The Neuralink team hopes the devices will correct injuries, bypass pain, record and restore memories, and enable telepathy. As Ballard and the Cronenbergs warned us, one person's mind-altering technology is another's absolute nightmare. "In Godflesh," Daniel Lukes writes, "the human is subsumed into the machine as an act of spiritual transubstantiation."[41] Computer processors open another path out of the body.

Answering Machines

"Welcome to the world of Pinecone Computers," Miles Harding (played by Lenny Von Dohlen) reads from a computer manual in *Electric Dreams* (1984). "This model will learn with you, so type your name and press Enter key to begin."[42] Since the big-screen tales of the 1980s PC-era, the idea of machines merging with humans has been a tenacious trope in popular culture. In *Tron* (1982) Kevin Flynn (played by Jeff Bridges) was sucked through a laser into the digital realm. Wired to the testosterone, the hormone-driven juvenile geniuses of *Weird Science* (1985) set to work making the woman of their dreams. *WarGames* (1983) famously pit suburban whiz-kids against a machine hell-bent on launching global

---

41 Daniel Lukes, "Black Metal Machine: Theorizing Industrial Black Metal," in *Helvete: A Journal of Black Metal Theory, Issue 1*, eds. Amelia Ishmael, Zareen Price, Aspasia Stephanou, and Ben Woodard (Earth: punctum books, 2013), 79.

42 Steve Barron (director), *Electric Dreams* [motion picture], written by Rusty Lemorande (Los Angeles: Virgin Films, 1984).

thermonuclear war. In *Electric Dreams* (1984), which is admittedly as much montage as it is movie, Miles (von Dohlen, who would go on to play the agoraphobic recluse Harold Smith in *Twin Peaks*, who kept obsessive journals of the townsfolks' innermost thoughts and dreams) attempts to navigate a bizarre love triangle between him, his comely neighbor, and his new computer.

Mechanical Matrimony

Where some see the whole mess of bodies and machines as one, big system. Others picture the airwaves themselves as extensions. "Telepresence," as envisioned by Pat Gunkel, Marvin Minsky, and others, sets out to achieve a sense of being there, transferring an embodied experience across space via telephone lines, satellites, and sensory feedback loops.[43] It sounds quaint in world where working from home is normal for many and at least an option for others, but McLuhan was writing about it in the 1960s, and Minsky and his lot were working on it in the 1970s.

Still others imagine a much more deliberate merging of the biological and the mechanical, postulating an uploading of human consciousness into the machines themselves. Known in robotic and artificial intelligence circles as "The Moravec Transfer," its namesake, the roboticist Hans Moravec, describes a human brain being uploaded, neuron by neuron, until it exists unperturbed inside a machine.[44] But Moravec wasn't the first to imagine such a transition. The cyberpunk

---

43 See Marvin Minsky, "Telepresence," *OMNI Magazine*, June 1980, 45–52.

44 See Hans Moravec, *Mind Children: The Future of Robot and Human Intelligence* (Cambridge: Harvard University Press, 1988). For

novelist and mathematician Rudy Rucker outlined the process in his 1982 novel, *Software*. "It took me nearly a year to really figure out the idea," he writes, "simple as it now seems. I was studying the philosophy of computation at the University of Heidelberg, reading and pondering the essays of Alan Turing and Kurt Gödel."[45] Turing was an early inventor of computing systems and AI, best known for the Turing test, whereby an AI is considered to be truly thinking like a human if it can fool a human into thinking so. Gödel was a logician and mathematician, best known for his incompleteness theorem. Both were heavily influential on the core concepts of computing and artificial intelligence. "It's some serious shit," Rucker writes of the process. "But I chose to present it in cyberpunk format. So, no po-faced serious, analytic-type, high literary mandarins are ever gonna take my work seriously."[46] In Rucker's story, a robot saves its creator by uploading his consciousness into a robot.

NASA's own Robert Jastrow wrote in 1984 that uploading our minds into machines is the be-all of evolution and would make us immortal. He wrote,

At last the human brain, ensconced in a computer, has been liberated from the weakness of the mortal flesh. [...] The machine is its body; it is the machine's mind. [...] It seems to me that this must be the mature form of intelli-

---

another early example, see G. Harry Stine, "The Bionic Brain," *OMNI Magazine*, July 1979, 84–86, 121–22.

45 Rudy Rucker, "Outer Banks & New York #1," *Rudy's Blog*, August 2, 2015, http://www.rudyrucker.com/blog/2015/08/02/outer-banks-new-york-1/.

46 Ibid.

gent life in the Universe. Housed in indestructible lattices of silicon, and no longer constrained in the span of its years by the life and death cycle of a biological organism, such a kind of life could live forever.[47]

Brick Body Kids Still Daydream[48]

In the desert along the border between California and Nevada, corporations are building server farms, giant structures meant to house machines instead of humans. These buildings don't look much different from any other nondescript industrial space from the outside, but they don't look like traditional buildings on the inside. They are unwelcoming, with little to offer humans. "For the employees there are only small rooms to relax in," says the architect Rem Koolhaas.

> They are paneled with Norwegian wood and Buddha statues—a debased kind of humanism, if you will: A little bit of mysticism, a little bit of warmth. But not too much of anything.

In the face of these buildings without bodies, Koolhaas also adopts a systems view, that "the need for human comfort can be very limiting when it comes to the design of buildings."[49] These descriptions evoke the inhuman, industrial enclaves of

47 Robert Jastrow, *The Enchanted Loom: Mind in the Universe* (New York: Simon & Schuster, 1984), 166–67.

48 Open Mike Eagle, *Brick Body Kids Still Daydream* [LP] (Tucson: Mello Music Group, 2017).

49 Quoted in Johannes Bohme, "An Interview with Rem Koolhaas," *The Believer*, January 31, 2020.

Broadrick's native Birmingham, as well as the lyrics the God-flesh song, "Curse Us All": "You're an empty shell / Built from brick / A living hell / Spewing shit."[50]

I am admittedly a lapsed student of AI, having dropped out of the University of Georgia's Artificial Intelligence Masters program midway through my first semester there in 1999. My interest in AI lies in the weird ways that consciousness and creation butt heads in the midst of such advanced technologies. If bodies didn't exist, we would have to invent them. Hans Moravec writes that

a human would likely fare poorly in such a cyberspace. Unlike the streamlined artificial intelligences that zip about, making discoveries and deals, rapidly reconfiguring themselves to efficiently handle changing data, a human mind would lumber about in a massively inappropriate body simulation, like a deep-sea diver plodding through a troupe of acrobatic dolphins. Every interaction with the world would first be analogized into a recognizable quasiphysical form: other programs might be presented as animals, plants, or demons, data items as books or treasure chests, accounting entries as coins or gold. Maintaining the fictions will increase the cost of doing business and decrease responsiveness, as will operating the mind machinery that reduces the physical simulations into mental abstractions in the human mind.[51]

---

50 Godflesh, *A World Lit Only by Fire* [LP] (London: Avalanche Recordings, 2014).

51 Hans Moravec, "The Senses Have No Future," in *The Virtual Dimension: Architecture, Representation, and Crash Culture*, ed. John Beckmann (New York: Princeton Architectural Press, 1998), 94.

We are the ghosts in these machines.[52] Our merging nuptials, to have, to hold, and to haunt. Given a choice between the physical and the digital, many of us would go ones-and-zeros in a final heartbeat. Perhaps we will anyway.[53]

52 Mark Fisher wrote, "there are ghosts in the machine, and we are they, and they are we." Mark Fisher, *The Weird and the Eerie* (London: Repeater Books, 2016), 109.

53 As Terence McKenna put it to Erik Davis, "the best answer I've gotten yet is out of Don DeLillo's *Underworld*, where the nun discovers that when you die you become your Web site." Quoted in Erik Davis, "Terrence McKenna's Last Trip," *WIRED*, May 1, 2000, https://www.wired.com/2000/05/mckenna/.

5

RAPTURE

Through Grace and Time

"I am as a mosquito lost at night over the Pacific Ocean. And the real Pacific Ocean that was once so endless — I can see it still down there as but the shining cheek of a world that has fallen from my feet. My aloneness is breath-taking."

— Guy Murchie, *Music of the Spheres*[1]

"The Rapture and the Singularity share one thing in common: they can never be verified by the living."

— Jaron Lanier, *You Are Not a Gadget*[2]

"In the church of my heart, the choir's in flames."

— Vladimir Mayakovsky, "A Cloud in Trousers"[3]

---

1   Guy Murchie, *Music of the Spheres,* 4.
2   Jaron Lanier, *You Are Not a Gadget: A Manifesto* (New York: Alfred A. Knopf, 2010), 26.
3   Vladimir Mayakovsky, "A Cloud in Trousers," in *Russian Poetry: The Modern Period*, eds. John Glad and Daniel Weissbort (Iowa City: University of Iowa Press, 1978), 14.

As if tuned to the mourning tones of some celestial mono-chord, Tom G. Warrior's guitar thunders like planets wobbling off their axes, ripped from their orbits. Warrior has helmed pioneering proto-black metal bands Hellhammer and Celtic Frost, as well as the more recent and more experimental Trip-tykon. On Celtic Frost's "A Dying God Coming into Human Flesh," the first single from their 2006 comeback record, *Mono-theist*, bassist Martin Ain sings, "frozen is heaven and frozen is hell, and I am dying in this living human shell" before Warrior comes in to wail the refrain, "I am a dying god coming into human flesh,"[4] over and over into the outer rings.

The Rapture, the leaving of Earth through heavenly sal-vation, is played out here in reverse, a divine degradation. Instead of a dying god caged in human flesh, in Rapture, the corporeal body is left behind for the eternity beyond. "I heard someone once say that 'music is the voice of God,'" Godflesh's Justin Broadrick says.

> In that sense, it's something that can get inside of you and move you spiritually on a communication level. The word "God" conjures something immense and inconceivable. The "flesh" part is what affects you on a physical level.[5]

---

4   Martin Eric Ain, "A Dying God Coming into Human Flesh," on *Monotheist* [LP], recorded by Celtic Frost (Dortmund: Century Media Records, 2006). The sentiment here recalls Thomas Ligot-ti's contention that God created humans as a form of suicide. See Thomas Ligotti, *The Conspiracy Against the Human Race* (New York: Hippocampus Press, 2010), 19.

5   Quoted in "FAQ," Godflesh.com, https://godflesh.com/faq.html. Eugene Thacker writes, "Being in the middle, as it were, the demon brings together the highest and the lowest, transforming the human

Extreme sounds at extreme volumes, like those performed by bands like Celtic Frost and Godflesh, bypass the brain and affect the body directly. In a statement Warrior and Ain would certainly agree with, Broadrick adds, "our music is loud and destructive."[6]

Only Death is Real: Celtic Frost. Photo by Sergio Archetti.

In theorizing such a spiritual sound, a "celestial mono-chord," seventeenth-century English occult philosopher

---

into a beast, and the beast into a god. The demon's metaphysical principle is 'meat.'" Eugene Thacker, *In the Dust of This Planet: Horror of Philosophy*, Volume 1 (Winchester: Zer0 Books, 2011), 116.

6   Ibid. Broadrick has cited "Anything is Mine" from Godflesh's *Selfless* as a "blatant Celtic Frost" rip-off. See Albert Mudrian, "Godflesh's Justin Broadrick: 'I Never Feel Comfortable at Any Festival,'" *Decibel Magazine*, October 17, 2018, https://www.decibelmagazine.com/2018/10/17/godfleshs-justin-broadrick-i-never-feel-comfortable-at-any-festival.

Robert Fludd's aim was not only to sonically order the cosmos but also to establish a god-sound preceding all others. Adam McLean terms Fludd's idea "hermetic," writing:

the hermetic world view held by such as Robert Fludd, pictured a great chain of being linking our inner spark of consciousness with all the facets of the Great World. There was a grand platonic metaphysical clockwork, as it were, through which our inner world was linked by means of a hierarchy of beings and planes to the highest unity of the Divine.[7]

The eleventh treatise of the *Corpus Hermeticum* declares that "unless you make yourself equal to god, you cannot understand god."[8] In his own book *Techgnosis: Myth, Magic, and Mysticism in the Age of Information*, Erik Davis describes the *Hermetica* as

an esoteric patchwork of alchemical, astrological, and mystical writings compiled from the second to the fourth centuries C.E., the *Hermetica* was mythically considered to be a single work composed by [...] Hermes Trismegistus.[9]

---

7   Adam McLean, "Quantum Consciousness," *Alchemy Web Site*, https://www.alchemywebsite.com/quantum.html.

8   Brian R. Copenhaver, trans., *Corpus Hermeticum* (Cambridge: Cambridge University Press, 1992), 41.

9   Erik Davis, *Techgnosis: Myth, Magic, and Mysticism in the Age of Information* (New York: Harmony, 1998), 27.

In 1617 Fludd wrote,

From the symphonious influence on the heavens, then it arises that the magnet attracts iron, amber silver, the sea-crab (*carabe*), hairs and straw, and the magnetic salve the nature of a wounded man, each holding the other in extraordinary affection. Their dissonant influence also produces the antipathy and discord of things, such as between lamb and wolf, dormouse and cat, the cock's crow and the lion, the sight of basilisk or *catablepas* and man, and many others. Now the concords of divine music draw similar things to them for their protection, and the discords of the same drive away and put to flight dissimilar and contrary things for the same purpose.[10]

And what are the lumbering dead but the leftover meat of transcendence, the cast-off husks of rapture? The spirit resides more in the head than the heart.[11] The zombie is the result of the mind permanently leaving the body on a lower plane.[12] Space-time doesn't ground; it suspends.[13] In

---

10 Fludd, "On the Occult and Wondrous Effects of Secret Music," in *Tractatus Apologeticus Integritatum Societatis de Rosea Crucis defendens* (Leiden, 1617). See also Eugene Thacker, "Sound of the Abyss," in *Melancology: Black Metal Theory and Ecology*, ed. Scott Wilson (Winchester: Zer0 Books, 2014), 182.

11 Smith, *The Body*, 297.

12 The ethnobotanist Wade Davis writes that a zombie "is a body without a complete soul, matter without morality."; *The Serpent and the Rainbow* (New York: Touchstone, 1985), 187.

13 See Kirk J. Schneider, *Horror and the Holy: Wisdom-Teachings of the Monster Tale* (Chicago: Open Court, 1993), esp. 9–11.

Fludd's view, these bodies are no longer led by the life-giving music of the cosmos, radio antennae sucked up by the signal, receivers received at last.

High-Rise[14]

Belief in aliens is often used as a trope in television shows and movies to signify instability or insanity. The hundreds of accounts available consist largely of unverifiable evidence and arguments that are shaky at best. Many of the reporters of alien phenomena seek to find them. Their seeking is "wishful thinking" in the words of Carl Jung.[15] Yet, in his one book on the subject, *Flying Saucers*, Jung admits that "a purely psychological explanation is illusory, for a large number of observations point to natural phenomenon, or even a physical one."[16] He adds, "something is seen, but we don't know what."[17] The witnesses fall into a few distinct categories: those prone to fantasy and self-delusion (of course), those who are awake and outdoors at odd hours (security staff and police officers), and those attuned to the skies (pilots and air traffic controllers).

The descriptions in the many reports I've read seem either embellished or evasive, imbued with insistence depending on how much the witness wants to believe. Often they're just repeating what they've seen or heard from movies, media, or others, what the anthropologist

---

14 J.G. Ballard, *High-Rise: A Novel* (London: Jonathan Cape, 1975).

15 Carl G. Jung, *Man and His Symbols* (New York: Bantam, 1964), 69.

16 Carl G. Jung, *Flying Saucers: A Modern Myth of Things Seen in the Skies* (Princeton: Princeton University Press, 1978), 132.

17 Ibid., 136.

Susan Lepselter calls "resonant apophenia."[18] There's just no way to tell if anyone has actually seen anything. The very designation "unidentified flying object" is so ambiguous as to be nearly useless. The Condon Report from 1969, the culmination of all of the Air Force's investigations into so-called sightings—Project Sign, Project Grudge, Project Blue Book—defines a UFO as follows:

> an unidentified flying object is here defined as the stimulus for a report made by one or more individuals of something seen in the sky (or an object thought to be capable of flight but seen when landed on earth) which the observer could not identify as having ordinary natural origin, and which seemed to him [sic] sufficiently puzzling that he [sic] undertook to make a report of it.[19]

In filing the report, one is saying that the sighting was "sufficiently puzzling" enough to file the report. It's not so much defining what a UFO is as it's defining what filing the report means. The Air Force either took the reports seriously enough or just received so many of them that they had to make them the subject of several official projects. Ex-Project Blue Book member Fritz Werner (not his real name) said in an interview that Blue Book existed because the Air Force "was getting too much publicity and there were too many people, other than official people

18 Susan Lepselter, *The Resonance of Unseen Things* (Ann Arbor, MI: University of Michigan Press, 2016), 19.
19 Edward Condon, *Final Report of the Scientific Study of Unidentified Flying Objects* (New York: Dutton, 1969), 9.

seeing things and reporting them."[20] Resonant apophenia indeed.

Upon allegedly returning from other planets, many early alien contactees believe they've been bestowed a mission to save this one. The earliest cases, the messages had to do with advancing technology to aid in our survival. Given the onset of the Cold War, contactees from the 1950s were increasingly "concerned with the effects of atomic power, war, pollution, and the need for the human family to come together."[21] Some were even touted as new messiahs, sent to save us all from our own, self-styled destruction.

In the case of cults like Heaven's Gate, UFO enthusiasts build religions around their search for truth. Balch and Taylor's germinal 1976 *Psychology Today* article "Salvation in a UFO" describes Heaven's Gate members as "metaphysical seekers": "before joining [Heaven's Gate], members of the UFO cult had organized their lives around the quest for truth. Most defined themselves as spiritual seekers."[22] In and out of other such groups before settling with Heaven's Gate, the founders and members could all be described as seekers. In his book *Heaven's*

---

20 Quoted in Kevin D. Randle, *A History of UFO Crashes* (New York: Avon Books, 1995), 58.

21 J. Gordon Melton, "The Contactees: A Survey," in *The Gods Have Landed: New Religions from Other Worlds*, ed. James R. Lewis (Albany: University of New York Press, 1995), 8. See also Curtis G. Fuller, *Proceedings of the First International UFO Congress* (New York: Warner Books, 1980).

22 Robert W. Balch and David Taylor, "Salvation in a UFO," *Psychology Today* 10, no. 5 (October 1976): 60.

Gate: America's UFO Religion, Benjamin E. Zeller studies the subject through religious scholarship. Counter to the media's reports of Heaven's Gate's mass suicides in March of 1997, Zeller writes that they "envisioned the Earth not as merely something to graduate from, but something to hate, human bodies not merely things top evolve out of, but vehicles to willfully destroy through suicide."[23] They saw this destruction not as suicide, but as "graduation from an unwanted terrestrial existence on an unbearable planet in disagreeable bodies."[24] The belief that in synchronized suicide, they were to board a UFO following the Hale-Bopp comet to salvation came from the New Age arm of their religion.

> Heaven's Gate emerged out of two theological worlds: Evangelical Christianity and the New Age movement, particularly the element of the New Age movement concerned with alien visitation and extraterrestrial contact.[25]

Loosely speaking, UFO religions culminate in a cafeteria-style belief system: all-you-can-eat at one end and monastic abstinence at the other. No matter their diet, saviors imbued with special knowledge or unwitting

---

23 Benjamin E. Zeller, *Heaven's Gate: America's UFO Religion* (New York: NYU Press, 2014), 177.

24 Ibid., 178.

25 Ibid., 65. See also Mark Dery, *The Pyrotechnic Insanitarium: American Culture on the Brink* (New York: Grove Press, 1999), 247–57; D.W. Pasulka, *American Cosmic: UFOs, Religion, Technology* (Oxford: Oxford University Press, 2019).

cyborgs implanted with alien technology, abductees rarely entertain the option of being wrong.

Where Jung saw the UFO phenomenon as seekers longing for a more complete life, Michael Heim sees it as "technology sickness."[26] Heim posited Alternate World Syndrome (AWS) as the switching between virtual and real worlds highlights the merging of technology with the human species, an extremely alien feeling we have yet to assimilate. It's the ontological jet lag that comes from visiting or envisioning another, alien world.[27] Heim continues, echoing our concerns from last chapter: "the fascination and pain of the UFO phenomenon shows us only the first glimpse of our ultimate merger with technology."[28] As Douglas Rushkoff puts it in his book *Team Human*,

The ultimate goal of personal transcendence was to leave the sinful, temporary body behind and float as a free, perfected consciousness. All that prior consumption was just fuel for the rocket, and the regrettable destruction something to leave behind with the rest of physical reality.[29]

Sometimes when entities play, it's difficult to tell whether they're flirting or fighting.

---

26 Michael Heim, *Virtual Realism* (New York: Oxford University Press, 1998), 182.

27 See Michael Heim, *The Metaphysics of Virtual Reality* (Oxford: Oxford University Press, 1993).

28 Heim, *Virtual Realism*, 197.

29 Douglas Rushkoff, *Team Human*, New York: W.W. Norton, 2019, 162.

Fickle Senses

The human brain's relationship with reality is not as steadfast as we'd like to think. The slightest ripple in our expectations can send us off one of many available edges. In his book, *The Conspiracy Against the Human Race*, Thomas Ligotti paraphrases Peter Wessel Zapffe, writing,

> consciousness is connected to the human brain in a way that makes the world appear to us as it appears and makes us appear to ourselves as we appear—that is, as "selves" or as "persons" strung together by memories, sensations, emotions, and so on.[30]

Our consciousness is a cumulative collection of recollections, connections, habits, and hearsay. When the continuity of those connections is corrupted, we are set adrift.

In Robert Guffey's book *Chameleo* (2015), which connects heroin addiction and Homeland Security among other disparate things, his friend Dion has the continuity of his consciousness severely corrupted. Dion's reality is already shaky at best, so Guffey sets out to document and investigate the odd goings on around Dion. Quoting Theodore Sturgeon, Guffey says, "always ask the next question."[31] *Chameleo* turns on this very fulcrum: It is a series of next questions asked not necessarily until the questions are answered, but until all of the possibilities are exhausted.

Dion is followed, harassed, and interrogated by groups of people seen and unseen. Invisible little agents begin

---

30 Ligotti, *The Conspiracy Against the Human Race*, 25.
31 Robert Guffey, *Chameleo* (New York: O/R Books, 2015), 29.

infiltrating his home after he is taken in for questioning about a load of missing night-vision goggles he had nothing to do with. These diminutive, invisible people sometimes appear as aberrations in Dion's peripheral vision. Imagine the painting of railroad tracks on the tops of trains. If you're looking at the train from above, you only see the tracks—unless you're watching very closely. Project Chameleo is based on a much more technologically advanced version of this very concept: invisibility by adaptive camouflage, like a texture-mapped, technicolor chameleon, obscuring a moving body. That's one of the simplest examples of the alien technology in this complex and confounding tale. Like Robert Fludd's monochord, perhaps Heaven's Gate, Guffey's friend Dion, and our other seekers are just tuned in to an alien frequency unavailable to the rest of us, a channel of consciousness from beyond. As Dr. Lilly wrote in 1972,

Presumably, there are many, many states of tuning for transmission and for reception. There are many, many bands of energy to which one can tune. There are bands emitted primarily by humans and received by humans. There are bands transmitted sand received by nonhuman intelligences on this planet, which we may or may not be able to tune in on. There are bands transmitted and received by entities who are vastly larger than us and who reside in other parts of the galaxy. Some reception can be from planetary transmissions; some can be from stars, suns, dust clouds, and so forth; some can be from humanlike intelligence somewhere in the galaxy and some can be from appa-

ratus constructed by civilizations a thousand to a mil-
lion years more advanced in their science.[32]

As below, so above.[33]

---

32 John C. Lilly, *The Center of the Cyclone: An Autobiography of Inner
    Space* (New York: The Julian Press, 1972), 142–43.

33 See Nicola Masciandaro, "On the Mystical Love of Black Metal," in
    Floating Tomb: Black Metal Theory, eds. Nicola Masciandaro and
    Edia Connole (Milan: Mimesis, 2015), 103; Edia Connole, "Seven
    Propositions on the Secret Kissing of 333 Black Metal: OSKVLVM,"
    in *Mors Mystica: Black Metal Theory Symposium*, eds. Edia Connole
    and Nicola Masciandaro (London: Schism, 2015), 347.

6

DRUGS

Encounter Culture

"There are many, many more shades and colors to darkness than just black."

— Martin Eric Ain, Celtic Frost/Hellhammer[1]

"It was like breaking your own leg so people would understand why you limped."

— Jerry Stahl, *Permanent Midnight*[2]

"I'm dying."
"Is it blissful?"
"It's like a dream."
"I want to dream.
With you."

— Deafheaven, "Dream House"[3]

---

1   Quoted in Sam Dunn and Scott McFadyen (creators), *Metal Evolution,* episode 12, Toronto, Canada: Banger Films, 2011.

2   Jerry Stahl, *Permanent Midnight* (Port Townsend, WA: Process, 1995).

3   Deafheaven, *Sunbather* [LP] (Beverly, MA: Deathwish, Inc., 2013).

On top of the compound meanings of the word "Streetcleaner," "Godflesh" contains many connotations as well. "'Godflesh' is the American Indian term for peyote," Justin Broadrick says, "but that really is kind of a coincidence. It's a coincidence that suits me just fine though."[4] Drugs and debauchery were an early part of Broadrick's life. He elaborates,

> Early Godflesh was absolutely a product of my own environment, but it wasn't entirely the landscape outside the window, the concrete and the council estate; it was also to do with my childhood background, the way my mother was when I was young and what I was exposed to. I was exposed to drug-taking at an early age and a lot of intense partying. [...] When we formed Godflesh, I was only 18 or something and still learning to deal with a lot of frustration, anger, love, hate...[5]

Broadrick's emotions parallel Dr. John C. Lilly's when returning to his body from an early acid trip. "I cried when I came back and found myself trapped in a body," Dr. Lilly lamented. "I didn't even know whose body it was at first. It was the sadness of reentry. I felt squashed."[6] As a neuroscientist and psychoanalyst, Dr. Lilly was interested in exiting the body through the mind. "In the province of the mind there are no

---

4   Quoted in http://www.godflesh.com/FAQ
5   Quoted in Joseph Burnett, "Extreme Language: An Interview with Justin K. Broadrick," *The Quietus,* May 9, 2012, https://thequietus.com/interviews/jk-flesh-interview-justin-broadrick/.
6   Quoted in Judith Hooper, "Interview: John Lilly," *OMNI Magazine,* January 1983, 78.

limits," Dr. Lilly once wrote. "However, in the province of the body there are limits not to be transcended."[7]

Long before most common psychedelic substances had been synthesized, the psychologist William James wrote about his trying nitrous oxide in his book, *The Varieties of Religious Experience*, originally published in 1902:

> Depth beyond depth of truth seems revealed to the inhaler. This truth fades out, however, or escapes, at the moment of coming to; and if any words remain over in which it seemed to clothe itself, they prove to be the verist nonsense.[8]

Admitting that the memory persisted, he went on to say that our waking, rational consciousness is but one kind of consciousness.

Rosi Braidotti urges us to "move forward into multiple posthuman futures." She writes:

> We need an active effort to reinvent the academic field of the Humanities in a new global context and to develop an ethical framework worthy of our posthuman times. Affirmation, not nostalgia, is the road to pursue: not the idealization of philosophical meta-discourse, but the more pragmatic task of self-transformation through humble experimentation.[9]

---

7   John C. Lilly, *Programming and Metaprogramming in the Human Biocomputer: Theory and Experiments* (New York: The Julian Press, 1974).

8   William James, *The Varieties of Religious Experience* (New York: Random House, 1994), 422.

9   Rosi Braidotti, *The Posthuman* (Cambridge: Polity Press, 2013), 150.

And as the ethnobiologist Terence McKenna put it, "The real crucible of this research is the Self."[10] Lilly set out to release his Self, to mute his corporeal existence, to defy his earthbound master, to blaspheme his god, his flesh.

Altered States: GODFLESH's *Streetcleaner*

The image on the cover of *Streetcleaner* is a screenshot from Ken Russell's 1980 movie *Altered States*. The image, silhouettes of a forest of crucifixions set against a sky of fire, is from one of the hallucination sequences in the film.[11] Adapted from the novel by Paddy Chayefsky, the movie follows a scientist

---

10 Terence McKenna, *The Archaic Revival* (New York: HarperCollins, 1991), 55.

11 In the liner notes to the 2010 reissue of the record, Jonathan Selzer suggests that the image represents the dual themes of *Streetcleaner*: "endurance and purifying deliverance."

attempting to escape his body through his mind, using sensory-deprivation tanks and mind-expanding substances. It's loosely based on Dr. Lilly's life and research. Exploring the extremes of neurophysiology, biophysics, and electronics, Lilly experimented on himself with isolation tanks, LSD, and later, ketamine. The movie provided hours of acid-induced entertainment for the teenaged Broadrick. "Those sorts of trips we had, watching *Altered States* and *The Devils*, were such an influence on *Streetcleaner*..." he remembers.[12]

While Chayefsky also wrote the screenplay, he was so unhappy with Russell's film he removed his name from the project.[13] Regardless of their creators' differences or incompatible tones, Chayefsky's novel and Russell's movie both depict the destination of their inner journeys as a nightmare, as climbing into the box with Pandora's evils and curses. Dr. Lilly saw tanking as a salve for our mortal sleeves, as no less than the sublimation of the Self.[14]

---

12 Quoted in Nasrallah, "Justin Broadrick."

13 Janet Maslin writes in the *New York Times*, "It's easy to guess why he and Mr. Russell didn't see eye to eye. The direction, without being mocking or campy, treats outlandish material so matter-of-factly that it often has a facetious ring. The screenplay, on the other hand, cries out to be taken seriously, as it addresses, with no particular sagacity, the death of God and the origins of man"; *New York Times,* December 25, 1980, Section 1, 15.

14 This "sublimation" is what Freud referred to as "alloplastic" (external) compensation or manipulation; See Norman O. Brown, *Life Against Death: The Psychoanalytical Meaning of History* (Middletown, CT: Wesleyan University Press, 1959), 170; Mary Douglas, *Purity and Danger: An Analysis of the Concepts of Pollution and Taboo* (London: Routledge & Keegan Paul, 1966), 116–18.

One in the Chamber

Sensory-deprivation tanks are lightless boxes. The shallow water inside is saturated with enough salts to keep a body buoyant. The air and water are kept at a humid, human temperature. Nothing to see. Nothing to hear. Nothing to feel. Total isolation from sense data. Total isolation from everything else except your Self.

"The tank is an awareness tool," said Lilly in 1980, "like meditation, like Gestalt, like psychosynthesis, like psychotherapy, like a hammer or a saw, and I find tank work, like any of the above tools, to be effective to the extent that I familiarize myself and practice with it. The tank assists a very simple function: It allows us to expand our awareness of our internal state of being, of our internal flow."[15] Without physical stimuli, the brain begins to improvise. Without practice, its improvisations can run astray.[16]

Paddy Chayefsky described his own isolation-tank experience as "a warm return to your mother's womb."[17] Similar to what some have called "the prisoner's cinema,"[18] the *OMNI Magazine* writer John Gorman describes his inner visit in 1980 differently:

---

15 Quoted in John Gorman, "Tanking," *OMNI Magazine*, August 1980, 62.

16 "Improvising" is how a doctor in the horror movie *Amityville 3-D* described a subject's mind during a lengthy tanking experience; David Ambrose (writer) and Richard Fleischer (director), *Amityville 3-D* [motion picture] (Los Angeles, CA: Orion Pictures, 1983).

17 David Itzkoff, *Mad as Hell: The Making of Network and the Fateful Vision of the Angriest Man in Movies* (New York: Times Books, 2014), 200.

18 See Oliver Sacks, *Hallucinations* (New York: Knopf, 2012).

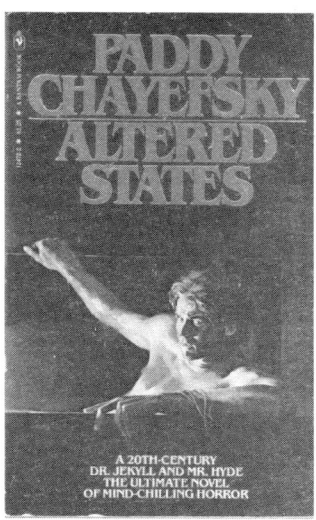

Out of body, out of mind: Paddy Chayefsky's *Altered States*, 1978

The darkness around me remains the same whether my eyes are open or closed. Still, it seems easier to close my eyes. At first, I feel time passing. My thoughts are logical and body centered. Will I become restless? Will I get scared and flee to daylight? But gradually my body recedes, and my thoughts grow random. Images come and go like a replay of recent events in my mind... Then those images, too, fade, replaced by a jumble of memories and dreamlike scenes.[19]

It took Dr. Lilly twenty-five years to convince his fellow scientists that tanking wouldn't drive people permanently

---

19 Gorman, "Tanking," 62.

out of their minds.[20] Before his first tank trip, Lilly had thirty-five years of school and eight years of psychoanalysis.[21] He knew his mind as much as he hated his body. Hans Moravec, the roboticist from Chapter Four, is not so convinced of these extra-bodily journeys. He writes,

> Humans need a sense of body. After twelve hours in a sensory-deprivation tank, floating in a totally dark, quiet, contactless, odorless, tasteless, body-temperature saline solution, a person begins to hallucinate, as the mind, like a television displaying snow on an empty channel, turns up the amplification in search of a signal, becoming ever less discriminating in the interpretations it makes of random sensory hiss. To remain sane, a transplanted mind will require a consistent sensory and motor image, derived from a body or from a simulation. Transplanted human minds will often be without physical bodies, but hardly ever without the illusion of having them.[22]

Dr. Lilly wasn't satisfied with just not having a body, though. He experimented with substances that would push his mind as far out of it as possible. He finally settled on what he called "Vitamin K," ketamine.[23]

---

20 Ibid.

21 Brown, "From Here to Alterity and Beyond," 207.

22 Moravec, "The Senses Have No Future," 93.

23 See Gorman, "Tanking."

Memories of the Future[24]

Ketamine is classified as a "dissociative anesthetic."[25] If floating in a tank that stifles one's senses didn't already divide them, ketamine forces a chemical wedge between the mind and the body. Dr. Ralph Metzner met with Dr. Lilly many times in the 1960s, 1970s, and 1980s, and followed his experiments closely. He writes that "ketamine expanded my consciousness into an abstract realm of thoughts and images, but without any of the sensory fireworks of the classic psychedelics and without their potential for dramatic emotional upheavals."[26] According to a mutual friend of Lilly's and Metzner's, Dr. Lilly preferred the out-of-body states that ketamine afforded because his "puritanical parents" had taught him to hate his own body. The seeds for bodily escape were planted early in the young Lilly, and they never ceased to bloom. At one point, Metzner was told by an emergency physician who worked with Dr. Lilly that Lilly was using ketamine multiple times a day: "He told me that John claimed he was 'channeling' extraterrestrial and extra-dimensional entities—but also occasionally the evening news."[27] The physician cut all contact with Lilly at this point. Lilly claimed to have had "encounters with super-human

---

24 This was Erich von Däniken's original title for his classic book *Chariots of the Gods*; see Erich von Däniken, *Chariots of the Gods* (New York: Berkeley Books, 1999 [1970]), viii.

25 Ralph Metzner, "John Lilly and Ketamine: Some Personal Recollections," in *The Ketamine Papers: Science, Therapy, and Transformation*, eds. Phil Wolfson, M.D., and Glenn Hertelius, Ph.D. (San Jose, CA: Multidisciplinary Association for Psychedelic Studies, 2016), 48.

26 Ibid.

27 Ibid.

beings who told me to go back and learn what it means to be human."[28]

Another close friend of Dr. Lilly's, and a fellow "ketamaniac," the video-artist known as Brummbear described the dangers of the drug during his talk at Lily's memorial: "Taking ketamine is not just a flirt with death—it's a tantric fuck with death—all nine holes of your body participating—and it's not free!"[29] He goes on to say that the eventual price of the trip is your mind. Dr. Lilly was described by his peers as both playful and profound. With his wild eccentricities and soaring intellect, he annoyed as often as he enlightened. "The mind is not operating with cells alone," he told Karl Jansen. "It operates with subatomic particles. If I reduce my consciousness to the Planck length of 6.624×10^{-27}, I can go anywhere in the Universe."[30]

Do Dice Play God?

We have used metaphors and metonymies of the most advanced technologies and scientific phenomenon to explain consciousness as far back as the Greek philosophers, but the technology of their time, needing constant human intervention, offered little in the way of models for the mind.[31] Since then, we have compared cognition to the machinations of the

28 uoted in Karl Jansen, *Ketamine: Dreams and Realities* (San Jose, CA: MAPS, 2001), 65.

29 Quoted in Metzner, "John Lilly and Ketamine," 49.

30 Quoted in Jansen, *Ketamine: Dreams and Realities*, 65.

31 See George Lakoff, "The Contemporary Theory of Metaphor," in *Metaphor and Thought*, ed. Andrew Ortony (Cambridge, UK: Cambridge University Press, 1993), 202–51; Gerald Raunig, *A Thousand Machines* (New York: Semiotext(e), 2010); Anthony Wilden, *System*

clock, the steam engine, the radio, the radar, and the computer.[32] As Dr. Lilly hints at above, the latest metaphor lies in the deep mysteries of quantum mechanics.

Anyone who claims to understand the mind is mistaken. Anyone who says they understand quantum mechanics is lying. It's not just a lack of understanding that unites the two, but our trying to define the most complex and confounding areas of our existence. Just as Robert Fludd's god-sound remained at the poetic level of application, so too do the unknowable mechanics of the subatomic world. "There is no quantum world," the physicist Niels Bohr once declared. "There is only an abstract quantum physical description."[33] Our language outreaches our understanding, but it sets us on the path. We need a vocabulary first. Bohr continues: "It is wrong to think that the task of physics is to find out how nature is. Physics concerns what we can say about Nature."

The 2013 film *Coherence*, written and directed by James Ward Byrkit, depicts a dinner party that devolves into

---

and Structure: Essays in Communication and Exchange (New York: Tavistock, 1972).

32 See Simon Penny, *Making Sense: Cognition, Computing, Art, and Embodiment* (Cambridge, MA: The MIT Press, 2017); P.A. Vroon, "Man-Machine Analogs and Theoretical Mainstreams in Psychology," in *Current Issues in Theoretical Psychology*, eds. W.J. Baker, M.E. Hyland, H. Van Rappard, and A.W. Staats (1987), 393–414.

33 Quoted in Karen Michelle Barad, *Meeting the Universe Halfway: Quantum Physics and the Entanglement of Matter and Meaning* (Durham, NC: Duke University Press, 2007), 254; see also Aage Petersen, "The Philosophy of Niels Bohr," *Bulletin of the Atomic Scientists* 19, no. 7 (1963): 8–14.

quantum weirdness and suspicion after a comet passes closely by overhead. The eight dinner guests meet multiple versions of themselves, get swapped and mixed between houses, and distrust each other in rotating cliques, all due to a comet-induced split of realities and quantum decoherence. The lead character, Em (Emily Foxler), goes so far as to peek into other houses to see how the night is playing out among her and her friends' other selves, eventually attempting to replace herself in a different reality. Incidentally, just like Sam Bell in *Moon*, Em is finally confronted by her other self as a voice on the phone. A minor concern in the film is the presence of a vial of ketamine.

Playing roulette with reality: Em and the quantum
chaos of *Coherence*, 2013

"You can drop it into some water, just to take the edge off," Beth (Elizabeth Gracen) suggests. "I don't know, I'm offering. It's not medication. It has passionflower, a little valerian, and a little... ketamine." She hesitates to reveal the K, and Mike (Nicholas Brendon), one of the other guests, immediately responds, "That's a horse tranquilizer!" Beth adds, "Yeah, but it's just a *whisper* of ketamine."[34] This dinner party doesn't travel "anywhere in the universe," but its members do experience some new possibilities. They attempt to keep it all straight with randomly numbered photographs, colored glowsticks, and totems. The mere mention of ketamine is enough to unground at least one of them, wandering off into other quantum lives.

Skepticism like Mike's remains the prevailing attitude toward consciousness-expanding and mind-altering substances, but proponents of their use swear by them. My friend Howard Rheingold has been using psychedelics since his mid-teens. He's written extensively on virtual reality, mobile technology, internet literacy, and other forms of what he calls "tools for thought." He describes his first LSD experience:

> I remember from my first trip, age 16, exploring the wonders of my fingertips, the feeling of breathing (taking in the universe and blowing it out), the feeling that my body is a robot commanded by my mind, experiencing my skin boundary as semi-permeable, with all the outside world that enters and leaves with my breath, the way my nerves

---

34 Writer/Director James Ward Byrkit tells me, "The *whisper* is what makes the concoction dangerous/mysterious/potent/magical/ useful. But she had to say it that way to make it sound like it was also safe and recreational. We wanted the ketamine to serve double duty—one, to provide a possible explanation of the strange communal meltdown that was occurring at the party (and pulling everyone into the kitchen so that Hugh and Amir could be alone in the living room and escape with the box), and two, as a way for Em to knock herself out without killing herself." Email with the author, October 4, 2021.

transmit sensations when I grasp something—so I wasn't separated from my boundary, not did I transcend its limits, but experienced a profound new understanding of the dance of outside-body and inside-body.[35]

He also told me about the overall influence of psychedelics on his thinking:

To a significant extent, my life path and my ways of thinking were permanently altered by my experimentation with psychedelics in my teens and twenties. In my sixties, the most important takeaway was that the revelations that had shaped my ways of thinking and living still seemed valid. Among these were the understanding that the universe (as JBS Haldane put it) is not only stranger than I imagine, but stranger than I can imagine (which makes me an agnostic on matters such as God and extrasensory experience); the direct experience of the way mind and culture construct reality—and the infinite number of other ways it can be constructed (as William James put it: "Our normal waking consciousness, rational consciousness as we call it, is but one special type of consciousness, whilst all about it, parted from it by the filmiest of screens, there lie potential forms of consciousness entirely different"). The possibility that consciousness, like energy and matter, is fundamental; that is, just as life seems to vivify matter and consciousness seems to add another dimension to sentient life, psychedelic experience put me in touch with a way of experiencing consciousness that seemed to be extending this teleology—and which implied that there are even

35 Email to the author, March 15, 2021.

more extended forms of consciousness, perhaps to come, perhaps coextant with the world we know but not perceptible to the unawakened mind; direct experience of the interbeing of all things.[36]

As Mark Pilkington reminds us, "We would all do well, however, to listen to Dr. Lilly's '11th Commandment', put forward in *The Deep Self* (1977): 'Thou shalt not bore god or he will destroy your universe.'"

---

36 Ibid.

7

DEATH

The End of an Error

"Fatality is the hermeticism of cause and effect. In fatality, everything you do, whatever you do, always leads to a certain end, and ultimately to the end—though that end, or the means to that end, remain shrouded in obscurity."

— Eugene Thacker, *Cosmic Pessimism*[1]

"At times I thought that only by self-destruction could I hope to cheat the relentlessly advancing assassins who were in me, in my eardrums, in my pulse, in my skull."

— Charles Kinbote, in Vladimir Nabokov's *Pale Fire*[2]

"And I find it kinda funny
I find it kinda sad
The dreams in which I'm dying
Are the best I've ever had."

— Tears for Fears, "Mad World"[3]

---

1   Eugene Thacker, *Cosmic Pessimism* (Minneapolis: Univocal Publishing, 2015), 14.

2   Vladimir Nabokov, *Pale Fire* (New York: Putnam, 1962), 97.

3   Tears for Fears, "Mad World," on *The Hurting* [LP] (New York: Mercury Records, 1983).

Prior to diving into the depths of inner space with Lilly and *Altered States*, Paddy Chayefsky wrote *Network*, the movie he's probably best known for. Even if you know nothing about it, you might know that newsman Howard Beale was mad as hell, and he wasn't going to take it anymore! This 1976 satire of network news has lost a lot of its bite over the years due to its prescience of television programming in the meantime, but the following exchange during a pitch meeting still has teeth:

> MAX
> We could make a series out of it.
> Suicide of the Week. Hell, why
> limit ourselves? Execution of the
> Week – the Madame Defarge Show!
> Every Sunday night, bring your
> knitting and watch somebody get
> guillotined, hung, electrocuted,
> gassed. For a logo, we'll have
> some brute with a black hood over
> his head. Think of the spin-offs
> – Rape of the Week –

> HOWARD
> (beginning to get caught up in the idea)
> Terrorist of the Week?

> MAX
> Beautiful!

> HOWARD
> How about Coliseum '74? Every

week we throw some Christians
to the lions! –

MAX

Fantastic! The Death Hour! I
love it! Suicides, assassinations,
mad bombers, Mafia hitmen, murder
in the barbershop, human sacrifices
in witches' covens, automobile
smashups. The Death Hour! A
great Sunday night show for the
whole family. We'll wipe fucking
Disney right off the air —

Human culture has been deeply interested in murder and the macabre since ancient ghost stories and monster tales. From the late-1960s to the early 1980s, the serial killer craze raged with headline after headline, from the Manson Family in Hollywood to Ted Bundy in Washington State, from John Wayne Gacy in Chicago to the Atlanta Child Murders. "Serial killers are a phenomenon almost no one understands," writes Dr. Joel Norris.

The killer rarely fits a single stereotype, his crimes are so "unreasonable" because the motive is internal, not explicit, and he is motivated by animal lust. Therefore, the serial killer's crimes always seem incomprehensible to reasonable people.[4]

---

4   Joel Norris, *Henry Lee Lucas: The Shocking True Story of America's Most Notorious Serial Killer* (New York: Zebra, 1991), 270–71.

Stuck in some formative, Freudian stage of fucked, serial killers are linked by their pathologies more than their beliefs, with appetites as insatiable as their fans. As Henry Lee Lucas put it, "Ain't never going to be a shortage of necks and knives."[5]

From Dahmer and *Dexter* to Hannibal Lector and *Hannibal*, we've made celebrities of serial killers and created characters based on them. "Running amok is a way of re-establishing one's reputation as a man to be feared and respected," writes Franco "Bifo" Berardi in his book *Heroes: Mass Murder and Suicide*, "but is also a way of escaping the world when life has become intolerable, and generally culminates in suicide."[6] We romanticize both aspects of this killing instinct, the nihilistic power-grab and the ultimate escape. It's a middle finger to everyone near and far, a fuck-the-world on both the grandest and the most intimate scales. The body is both actor and enemy. If the flesh is their god, they are devoted to destroying it. Berardi continues, "When running amok, the borders between one's body and the surrounding universe are blurred, and so is the limit between killing and being killed."[7]

The Streetcleaner
The song "Night Shift" by Siouxsie and the Banshees sums it up nicely: "Fuck the mothers, kill the others / Fuck the others,

---

5 Quoted in Ryan Green, *Trust Me: The True Story of Confession Killer Henry Lee Lucas* (independently published, 2019), 63; Ted Bundy added, "What's one less person on the face of the earth, anyway?"; Quoted in Al Cimino, *Ted Bundy: America's Most Evil Serial Killer* (London: Arcturus, 2021), 239.

6 Franco "Bifo" Berardi, *Heroes: Mass Murder and Suicide* (New York: Verso, 2015), 55.

7 Ibid., 56.

kill the mothers / I'll put it out of my mind because... / I'm out of my mind with you / In heaven and hell with you..."[8] Any guilt we might have had becomes outrage as we scapegoat these killers with our latent murderous desires.[9]

The song is about Peter Sutcliffe, a.k.a. The Yorkshire Ripper, who terrorized the streets of England between 1975 and 1980. Mere weeks before he was arrested, Sutcliffe sent a poem to the *Sheffield Star* newspaper called "Clueless," a poem he signed "The Streetcleaner."[10] The poem is one of many sources Justin Broadrick references as possible inspiration for the name of the first Godflesh record. Sutcliffe adopted the name because he believed he was cleaning the streets of sin.

"My desire to kill prostitutes was getting stronger than ever and it took me over completely," he said after confessing his twelfth murder.[11] "I was in a dilemma I wanted to tell someone what I was doing but I thought about how it would affect my wife and family. I wasn't too much bothered for myself." He also described his mission to cleanse the streets of prostitution as God-given: "I'd been told what my mission was, like a soldier in a war. I couldn't disobey my orders. They came

---

8   Siousxie and the Banshees, "Night Shift," on *Juju* [LP] (London: Polydor, 1981).

9   See Gary J. Shipley, "Visceral Incredulity, or Serial Killing as Necessary Anathema," in *Serial Killing: A Philosophical Anthology*, eds., Edia Connole and Gary J. Shipley (London: Schism, 2015), 21–37.

10 See Nicole Ward Jouve, *"The Streetcleaner": The Yorkshire Ripper Case on Trial* (London: Marion Boyars, 1986), 214.

11 Quoted in Barbara Jones, *Voices from an Evil God: The True Story of the Yorkshire Ripper and the Woman Who Loved Him* (London: Blake Publishing, 1993), 2–4.

from the highest authority."[12] Sutcliffe went so far as to use the unorthodox legal defense of diminished responsibility on theological grounds.[13] One of the many books about Sutcliffe is called *Voices from an Evil God*, and he believed in his divine guidance. "God invested me with the means of killing," he said. "He has got me out of trouble, and I am in God's hands."[14]

' Clueless '

POOR OLD OLDFIELD
WORKED IN A COLDFIELD

HOBSON HAS NO CHOICE
MISLED BY A VOICE

RELEASE OF DRURY
AROUSES FURY

BRADFORD WAS NOT ME
BUT JUST WAIT AND SEE

SHEFFIELD WILL NOT BE MISSED
NEXT ON THE LIST
' The Streetcleaner'
(T. S.)

Signed, "The Streetcleaner"

---

12 Statement to Dr. Milne, read out in court during his trial. Quoted in *The Yorkshire Ripper*, http://www.execulink.com/~kbrannen/.

13 Ibid.

14 Ibid.

Save an abnormal need to cling to his mother's skirt, Sutcliffe is reported to have had a fairly normal childhood.[15] He started his six-year mission eliminating sex workers he saw sullying the streets of England in Leeds, Bradford, and Wakefield. Before he was caught, he became less discerning, killing seemingly at random: a university student, a sixteen-year-old shop girl, a nineteen-year-old building clerk. The largest manhunt in British law-enforcement history followed. He was ultimately found guilty of murdering thirteen women and attempting to murder seven more.[16]

Sutcliffe commented on his fifteenth murder, Yvonne Pearson,

> She said, "It's good timing, or you can put it down to fate." Unfortunately for her, I thought this was my direct signal... I had a hammer on the car floor, and she said very little after that. I took her to where she wanted to go and after I killed her, I apologized. I said I was sorry, and she could get up, and that she would be all right. She didn't, and I realized it was meant to be.[17]

The Hoax of Death

Where Peter Sutcliffe claimed that he heard the voice of God tell him to kill women, Henry Lee Lucas said he acted of his

---

15 Peter Vronsky, *Sons of Cain* (New York Berkeley, 2018).

16 See Roger Cross, *The Yorkshire Ripper: The In-Depth Study of a Mass Killer and his Methods* (London: HarperCollins UK, 1981), 144; Vronsky, *Sons of Cain*, 2018.

17 Ibid.; on November 13, 2020, Peter Sutcliffe died after refusing treatment for the COVID-19 virus.

own volition. At the beginning of the title track of Godflesh's *Streetcleaner*, there's a voice that says, "I didn't hear voices. It was a conscious decision on my part. With me it was more of a power thing because of my fantasies, I simply acted on my fantasies."[18] It's allegedly a clip from the hours of recordings of Lucas's confessions, who was either America's most prolific serial killer or its biggest troll.

Henry Lee Lucas provides a singular case study on how serial killers emerge from early childhood.[19] He was born in Blacksburg, Virginia, one of the most impoverished regions in the country, in 1937. Anderson, his alcoholic father, lost his legs after drunkenly falling on the railroad tracks in the path of a slow rolling train. He made money by skinning minks, selling pencils, and distilling moonshine. Anderson had Lucas drinking hard alcohol by age ten. His father died when Lucas was thirteen-years old, crawling out into the snow blind drunk and lying there until pneumonia killed him.[20]

Lucas's mother, Viola, beat him with anything she could get her hands on. She once hit Lucas so hard with a piece of wood that he was knocked out for three days. She dressed him as a girl on the first day of school, sending him off in a dress and curling his long hair. She regularly told him he was evil and that he would die in prison. Viola was a sex worker,

---

18 Godflesh, "Streetcleaner," on *Streetcleaner*; see also René Walczak, "Godflesh: Strength Through Purity," *Propaganda Magazine*, no. 19, (Fall 1992), 40.

19 Peter Vronsky writes, "Lucas's childhood history can serve as a manual on how to incubate a serial killer. It includes virtually every factor reported by different serial killers in one single life."; *Serial Killers* (New York: Berkeley, 2004), 276.

20 Ibid.

and he often witnessed her practicing the trade in their small dirt-floor cabin in the Virginia hill country. He claimed one of his earliest memories of her was a postcoital shooting of a patron in the leg with a shotgun, the blast spraying the man's blood on the young Lucas, permanently connecting physical violence, blood, and sex in his developing mind.[21]

Growing up in this environment has been evidence of not only Lucas's sexual deviance but also his hatred of sex workers in particular, hatred of women in general, and his many murders thereof. He once described a sickness overtaking his body as a boy:

> I didn't know anything happening around me. I couldn't hear, really. It was like being in a different world. I used to float through the air when I was a kid, too. I used to be layin' in bed, just felt like you're floatin' right off the bed up in the air. Just feel like I could fly. It's not a nice feeling. It's a weird feeling.[22]

The fact that Peter Sutcliffe and Henry Lee Lucas targeted sex workers is significant here—not only because both killers felt like they were doing God's work, performing a service for society, but also because in their trade, sex workers use their bodies. In selling flesh, their presence and practices highlight the value of fulfilling fleshly deeds and the weaknesses of bodily desires. We are all fragile and frail.

Once his body was locked behind bars, Lucas set out manipulating those around him. Prison provides the stability and control that serial killers often lack on the outside, where

---

21 Ibid.

22 Quoted in Norris, *Henry Lee Lucas*, 40–41.

they don't have any externally imposed structure. As Dr. Joel Norris puts it, the institution becomes their "personality skeleton."[23] Where the body is seen as a prison, here is the inverse: prison seen as the body.

Henry Lee Lucas became a cold-case clearinghouse as thousands of police officers, eager to close cases, came from all over the country to talk to him. Ex-Texas Ranger and Williamson County Sheriff Jim Boutwell and officer Bob Prince set up a task force to coordinate interviews and confessions in exchange for strawberry milkshakes, black coffee, and Pall Malls, the nonstop attention notwithstanding. Lucas leveraged the power of telling the lies everyone wants to believe. With the media as hungry for serial-killer stories to splash on their front pages as law enforcement was to clear murder cases off their growing dockets, Boutwell and Lucas became a team: the cop and the con man.

One of Lucas's many confabulations was a child-abducting, cannibalistic cult called the "Hand of Death." Feeding off the Satanic panic of the 1980s, during which metal bands were dragged into court for inciting murder and suicide with their lyrics,[24] he and his erstwhile road partner, Ottis Toole, supposedly did evil deeds, conducted business, and attended black masses in the name of this shadow organization, driven by "the demonic force of the universe":

What I seen with my own eyes, nobody's ever seen before. I seen the power of evil at work in the world, and I felt

---

23 Ibid., 301.

24 See, for instance, Mike Sager, "Fact: Five Out of Five Kids Who Murder Love Slayer," in *Revenge of the Donut Boys* (New York: Thunder's Mouth Press, 2007), 103–20.

it practiced through me. I came to believe that my own destiny was with the power of evil. It made me do things that today I wish I could undo, but I can't. I have to pay for what I done and confess what I done.[25]

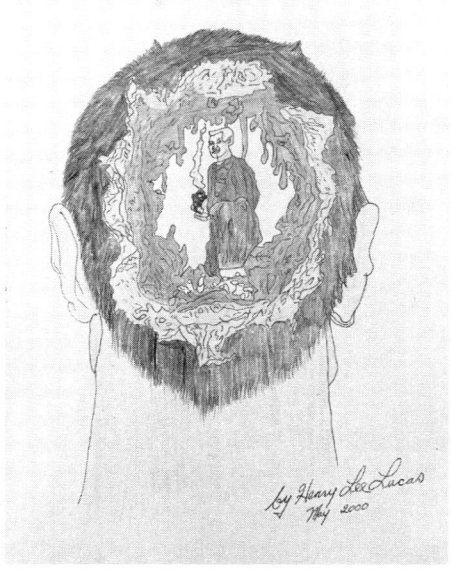

"Hole in the Head" by Henry Lee Lucas, 2000, colored pencil on cardstock.
Courtesy of the Graveface Museum, Savannah, Georgia

His friend and pastor in the Texas jail, Sister Clemmie, seeing only a sweet, tender man who enjoyed painting and studying the Bible with her, was convinced of his demonic possession. "Being in the middle, as it were," Eugene Thacker writes, "the

---

25 Quoted in Norris, *Henry Lee Lucas*, 99–100.

demon brings together the highest and the lowest, transforming the human into a beast, and the beast into a god. The demon's metaphysical principle is 'meat.'[26] The visceral vessel we inhabit, the body, is made of meat.

Confounding his legal counsel, Lucas was resolved to die at the hand of the state. After he killed his one true love, he sought nothing more than "salvation in his own death."[27] This rationale was his justification for confessing to murders he hadn't committed. If he killed himself, he wouldn't be allowed to join his girlfriend Becky Powell in heaven. If the state killed him, he'd be with her forever after. Lucas claims that a light came into the tiny Montague County jail cell that held him captive, urging him to confess his sins. "If you confess your sins to man, I will forgive you."[28] Once convicted of one murder, he toured the country confessing to multiple murders at every stop. He claimed God told him to, that it would be his path back out of the darkness.

While he seemed like law enforcement's best friend, he was really benefiting other murderers. Though the number varied wildly, Lucas claimed as many as 600 victims, but there were only three that had evidence beyond his confessions: his mom; his girlfriend, Becky; and his eighty-two-year-old landlord in Texas, Kate Rich. He was ultimately only convicted of eleven murders, mostly hitchhikers in Texas.[29] The Texas Rangers

---

26 Thacker, *In the Dust of This Planet,* 116.

27 Norris, *Henry Lee Lucas,* 281. Berardi describes the killers at Columbine as motivated by similar forces: "suffering people who committed mass murder with the intention of being killed in order to be released from the intolerable burden of their life." Berardi, *Heroes,* 95.

28 Ibid., 205, 251.

29 Vronsky, *Serial Killers,* 2004.

attributed 200 different murders to him. In the intervening years, only twenty of those have ever been passed on to other perpetrators.[30]

It's not to say that serial killing is strictly a part of the past, but cellphones, surveillance technology, and DNA evidence have put a damper on the phenomenon. Serial killing is longitudinal, targeting individual bodies over time. However, in the twenty-first century, mass murder has supplanted the serial killing of multiple single victims. One is breadth, the other depth. Serial killers amass bodies one by one, meticulously marking each one. Mass murderers make their impact all at once, like a bomb exploding. Given technological advances that make everyone with a phone a potential Zapruder, a mass killer goes in not expecting to get away with it, usually not even expecting to survive. A mass killer goes in to take out as many bodies as possible in one go, including their own. The stakes are different, and so are the tools.

Hostile Gospel

"Do you ever feel like there's a thousand people locked inside of you?"[31] Boxer Santeros (played by Dwayne Johnson) asks Roland Taverner (played by Sean William Scott) in Richard Kelly's *Southland Tales* (2006). "But it's your memory that keeps them glued together, keeps all those people from fighting one another. Maybe in the end that's all we have: the memory gospel." Memory also plays an important part in Kelly's first movie, *Donnie Darko* (2001). At the height of my fandom of

---

30 In 1998, then governor George W. Bush commuted Lucas's one death sentence to a life term. He died in prison on March 12, 2001.

31 Richard Kelly (writer and director), *Southland Tales* [motion picture] (Los Angeles: Universal, 2006).

the film, I attended a midnight screening of the director's cut at the Egyptian Theatre in Seattle. During the trivia contest that preceded the movie, I was asked to sit out due to my long string of correct answers. The movie struck something in me at a time when I needed to be struck. As Kelly himself put it, "I think you are challenged by things that are slightly beyond your grasp."[32] It is those things obscured that make a movie like this so engaging, endearing, and enduring.

Though he's never formally acknowledged it, Kelly's Frank the Rabbit character, a six-foot tall guy in a bunny suit who feeds Donnie cryptic messages throughout the film, can be interpreted as a play on the pookah legend, which Robert Anton Wilson explained as follows:

> The pookah takes many forms, but is most famous when he appears as a giant, six-foot white rabbit—which is the form most Americans know from the play and film, *Harvey*. Whatever form the pookah takes, he retains the special ability of his species, which is like that of Thoth in Egyptian legend, Coyote in Native American myth, or Hanuman the Divine Monkey in Hindu lore — he can move us from one universe, or Belief System, into another, and he likes to play games with our ideas about "reality."[33]

In his 2013 book *Look at the Bunny*, Dominic Pettman reads the rabbits in both John Steinbeck's *Of Mice and Men* (1937) and Richard Adams's *Watership Down* (1972) as pookah-like

---

32 Richard Kelly, "The Making of Southland Tales," on *Southland Tales* [DVD] (Los Angeles: Universal, 2006).

33 Robert Anton Wilson, *Cosmic Trigger, Volume II: Down to Earth* (Las Vegas: New Falcon, 1991), 29.

guides from the future. Skipping ahead, however, is not always a promising prospect. The Cassandra conundrum of seeing imminent catastrophe and having no one in the present believe you follows the prophet, rabbit or otherwise. The vagabond rabbits of *Watership Down*, led by the frequently hysterical Fiver; Lennie, George, and Candy in *Of Mice and Men*, led by a rabbit-ridden future vision; Donnie Darko, led by his daylight hallucinations of Frank; and Elwood, led by his imaginary Harvey, are all held suspect by their peers. "The list of lapine totems, no doubt, could go on and on—which is partly my point," Pettman writes.[34]

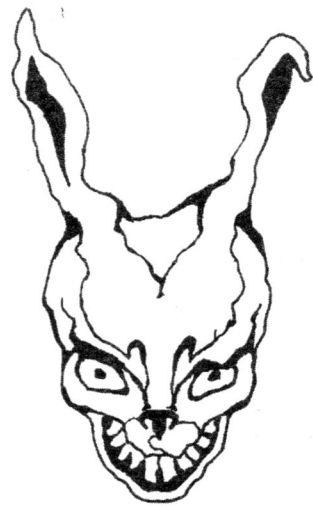

The Frank the Rabbit mask, as sketched by Richard Kelly

34 Dominic Pettman, *Look at the Bunny: Totem, Taboo, Technology* (London: Zer0 Books, 2013), 63.

The iconography of *Donnie Darko* starts with Frank. Like Jason Voorhees's hockey mask or Freddy Krueger's razor-fingered glove, Frank's rabbit suit is as distinctive a symbol for a movie as there has ever been. Frank is from the future, and he mentors Donnie through the film with cryptic guidance and disjointed advice. The setting and surroundings of Halloween, as well as the late-night bike ride nod to *E.T.* (1982), are also endemic to this movie. Unlike any other night of the year, Halloween holds unprecedented adolescent freedoms and fears, all hidden behind masks and costumes. In the midst of the musings of a confused, possibly schizophrenic teenage boy, *Donnie Darko* puts no less than the future of humanity at stake. Drawing from Graham Greene's "The Destructors" (1954), Adams' *Watership Down* (1972, the inspiration for Frank, according to Kelly), and Martin Scorsese's *The Last Temptation of Christ* (1988), he carries us to the absolute brink on All Hallow's Eve. The meaning of all of this is never fully explained, but whatever it means remains important to us. It's not enough to just like the characters and to wonder. We have to care. As Stephen Jay Gould once put it,

> We also need the possibility of cataclysm, so that, when situations seem hopeless, and beyond the power of any natural force to amend, we may still anticipate salvation from a messiah, a conquering hero, a *deus ex machina*, or some other agent with power to fracture the unsupportable and institute the unobtainable.[35]

---

35 Stephen Jay Gould, *Questioning the Millennium: A Rationalist's Guide to a Precisely Arbitrary Countdown* (New York: Crown, 1999), 58.

Rabbits are chosen as characters in stories because of their agility as tricksters as well as their status as prey.[36] They're able to cheat death for a time, but death always wins in the end. Death is a hunter that always gets its prey, even where humans are concerned. Justin Broadrick says, "I'm forever getting overwhelming messages from people saying, 'you saved my life.' It's brutal because I feel like I'm saving my own fucking life through this media."[37] Whether creating or destroying, we all wear the masks of death. We are perhaps most human when we're not here at all.

---

36 Pettman, *Look at the Bunny*. Susan E. Davis Margo Demello, *Stories Rabbits Tell* (New York: Lantern Books, 2003), 173.

37 Quoted in Poscic, "Out Demons Out," 33.

8

END

All the World's a Grave

"These premonitions of disaster remained with me. During my first days at home, I spent all my time on the veranda, watching the traffic move along the motorway, determined to spot the first signs of this end of the world by automobile, for which the accident had been my own private rehearsal."

— James in J.G. Ballard's *Crash*[1]

"Con men don't change, they break, shatter—explosions of matter in cold interstellar space, drift away in cosmic dust, leave the empty body behind."

– from William S. Burroughs' *Naked Lunch*[2]

"Through fiction we saw the birth
Of futures yet to come
Yet in fiction lay the bones, ugly in their nakedness
Yet under this mortal sun, we cannot hide ourselves"

— Isis, "In Fiction"[3]

---

1   Ballard, *Crash*, 50.
2   William S. Burroughs, *Naked Lunch* (New York: Grove Press, 1959), 11.
3   Isis, "In Fiction," from *Panopticon* [LP] (Los Angeles: Ipecac Records, 2012).

"My first love was science fiction films and the music that went along with them," Justin Broadrick says. "My next love was horror movies, and I became fixated with the brutal, dark, and brooding sounds that went along with those as well."[4] Godflesh's 2014 reunion record, their first release in over a decade, is called *A World Lit Only by Fire*. The title evokes a flaming planet, nations and nature scorched in ruin. It's actually a reference to a book by the same name by William Manchester about the darkness of the Middle Ages.[5] Both visions work well for Godflesh's sound: It's dark, brutal, and could have come from a tumultuous past or a post-apocalyptic future. The hard, cold sound could be made by bones or stones as easily as it could be bricks or concrete blocks.

"Have you ever participated in genocide?" was the question on one of the forms Broadrick filled out on his first trip to the States after 9/11. "I always said Godflesh was, to some extent, protest music. It comes from an anarcho-punk background," adding, "but after all the idealistic sloganeering and stuff, I sort of went the opposite way. I started to feel like the human race wasn't worth saving after all."[6] As he sings on "Life Giver Life Taker" from *A*

---

4   Quoted in Garth Ferrante, "Godflesh Explains Selfless' Song Titles," August 1994, https://godflesh.com/articles/int2.txt.

5   William Manchester, *A World Lit Only by Fire: The Medieval Mind and the Renaissance: Portrait of an Age* (New York: Little, Brown & Co., 1992).

6   Quoted in Jason Heller, "Justin Broadrick of Jesu," *AV Club*, April 5, 2007, https://film.avclub.com/justin-broadrick-of-jesu-1798211103.

World Lit Only by Fire: "The dying sun / Is all ours / It will reclaim / Our fallen earth."[7]

Future-minded science-fiction writers have recently been comparing the dearth of mentions of the twenty-second century so far in the twenty-first to the many mentions of the twenty-first at the same point last century.[8] It is as if we can't even imagine our future anymore, but dystopic doom was around back then, too. "I abhor humanity," Birkin says to Ursula in D.H. Lawrence's 1920 novel *Women in Love*. "I wish it was swept away. It could go, and there would be no absolute loss, if every human being perished tomorrow. The reality would be untouched. Nay, it would be better."[9] I distinctly remember an episode of *The Twilight Zone* I watched as a kid. It was called "Time Enough at Last," and starred the late Burgess Meredith. I don't remember all of it, just the end: There's a man, a bibliophile, he's the last person left on Earth, and he's ecstatic because he's surrounded by books, mounds and mounds of them. He finally breaks his reverie in order to get started reading. Then he breaks his glasses.

---

7   Godflesh, *A World Lit Only by Fire*.

8   See Abraham Riesman, "William Gibson Has a Theory About Our Cultural Obsession with Dystopias," *Vulture*, August 1, 2017, https://www.vulture.com/2017/08/william-gibson-archangel-apocalypses-dystopias.html; Benjamin Bratton and Bruce Sterling, "Bruce Sterling & Benjamin Bratton in Conversation," *SCI-Arc Channel*, 2018, https://www.youtube.com/watch?v=Z0__x5SG8WY.

9   D.H. Lawrence, *Women in Love* (New York: Thomas Seltzer, 1920), 143.

Burgess Meredith in *The Twilight Zone*, 1960

The trepidation of that tragic moment, recombinant with worries of the apocalypse, was a seed planted in my head. And more than any other Cold War-era image of imminent destruction splashed on the television during my childhood, the nerd in me nurtured that single idea: the apocalypse seemed inevitable, and it did not look like a particularly good time. In fact, it looked like a tailor-made, personal purgatory.

The rhetorical scholar Barry Brummett writes that apocalyptic orators claim special knowledge of a hidden order, to advise others to make great sacrifices on the basis of that knowledge, even to predict specific times and place for the end of the world.[10]

In spite of *The Twilight Zone* episode mentioned above, I've always considered myself more concerned with my own demise than with the end of the word, but the latter is clearly hanging heavy in the mass-mind. Brummett also writes that the strategy of apocalyptic rhetoric is "to respond to a sense of chaos and anomie, whether acute or potential, with reassurances of a plan that is ordering history."[11] Between looming pandemics, postponed human holocaust, and all the other examples of global weirding, there are certainly those who would have us believe that our doom is imminent. As far as the darker strains of heavy metal music are concerned, we deserve the anxiety, as it's likely our own fault.

Black Metallic[12]
Black metal's corpse-paint makeup and entropic rhythms give sight and sound to the grinding ghost of human civilization. More so even than the industrial pounding of Godflesh, black metal is what's left when the systems have all broken down. The writer and artist Evan Calder Williams sees the ethos of the genre as

---

10 Barry Brummett, *Contemporary Apocalyptic Rhetoric* (New York: Praeger, 1991), 87.

11 Ibid.

12 Catherine Wheel, "Black Metallic," from *Ferment* [LP] (Los Angeles: Fontana, 1992).

a battlefield from the start, as a phenomenal working through of that imagined site, that promised zone of contestation where the contemporary world is swept away to confront the old antagonisms.[13]

The battle is with the contemporary world itself. Often thought of as Satanic from the outside, orthodox black metal is typically just anti-religion, anti-Western, and longing for Norwegian Nationalism over some horned devil as such. As Gaahl, former lead vocalist of the Norwegian black metal band Gorgoroth, told Peter Beste, "I think Christianity has made people afraid of solitude; afraid of the idea of being alone."[14] Theirs is a call for the Old Norse ways and solitary contemplation, a return to the time before the Westernization of Scandinavia.

At barely thirty years old, black metal is a relatively young musical genre. Its roots running back to such theatrical and thrash acts as Hellhammer, Celtic Frost, Venom, Bathory, Mercyful Fate, and Slayer, it finally found fertile ground in Scandinavia in the late 1980s and early 1990s. This second wave, including such bands as Mayhem, Darkthrone, Burzum, and Emperor, is what most are referring to when they utter the words. As author Ulrike Serowy puts it, black metal is "music that touches the inmost depths, goes beyond words, music that conjures infinity."[15] The bands and fans all wear head-to-

---

13 Evan Calder Williams, *Combined and Uneven Apocalypse: Luciferian Marxism* (London: Zer0 Books, 2011), 131.

14 Quoted in Peter Beste, *True Norwegian Black Metal: We Turn in the Night Consumed by Fire* (New York: Vice Books, 2008), 107.

15 Ulrike Serowy, *Skogtatt: A Novella* (Lohmar, Germany: Hablizel, 2013), 33.

toe black leather, wrist- and arm-bands, and boots with spikes or nails, and black and white corpse paint.

Described as "the most widely demonized and vilified music scene in rock history," black metal took traditional metal to new extremes.[16] The major characters involved in Norway's second wave include Øystein Aarseth (a.k.a. Eronymous) of Mayhem, Per Yngve Ohlin (a.k.a. Dead) of Mayhem, Varg Vikernes (a.k.a. Count Grishnackh) of Burzum and Mayhem, and Bärd Eithun (a.k.a. Faust) of Emperor, among several others. "Dead's name was an ever-looming portent of his destiny" write Moynihan and Søderlind in their 1998 exposé of the scene, *Lords of Chaos*.[17] Very much into self-mutilation, often on stage, Dead eventually shot himself in the head with a shotgun. His bandmate Euronymous found the body, took pictures, and reportedly took pieces of his skull and brains. One of the pictures ended up as the cover art for the live Mayhem record, *Dawn of the Black Hearts*, and Euronymous supposedly made a stew out of Dead's brains and necklaces out of pieces of his skull.

The sometime bass player for Mayhem and full-time one-man-band Burzum, Grishnackh, paranoid about an alleged plot by Euronymous to kill him, beat him to the punch: One late night in Oslo, Grishnackh stabbed Euronymous to death. Euronymous had been the figurehead of the Norwegian black metal scene. His record store in Oslo, Helvete, had served as a

---

16 Andrew O'Hehir, "Sympathy for the Devil Worshipers," movie review of *Until the Light Takes Us*, Salon, December 7, 2009, https://www.salon.com/2009/12/07/until_the_light/.

17 Michael Moynihan and Didrik Søderlind, *Lords of Chaos: The Rise of the Satanic Metal Underground* (Port Townsend, WA: Feral House, 1998), 58.

central meeting place for bands and fans, as well as a place to buy records and paraphernalia. It was darkly lit, and Euronymous wanted it to be kept completely dark and to make customers use torches to see the records and their way around.

Underwhelmed by what he saw as posturing without action by Euronymous, Grishnackh allegedly set about burning down churches. Grishnackh's philosophy is one of nationalism. He sees Christianity as colonialist, having moved into Norway and displaced the native Norse religion. His intentions did not keep the church burnings from being seen as "Satanically motivated" by the media. The heavy metal magazine *Kerrang!* ran a cover story that read, "Arson... Death... Satanic Ritual... The Ugly Truth about Black Metal" and the spread bore the quotation, "We are but slaves of the one with horns..." across the top of its pages.

> Copycat church attacks followed throughout the Northern Hemisphere, often accompanied with spray-painted pentacles and 666's and so forth, and whatever had once been distinctive about the Norwegian scene just became, in Vikernes' [Grishnackh] words, "a bunch of brain-dead, heavy-metal guys."[18]

The image of the black metal scene at large is one of darkness and evil. Dick Hebdige writes,

> In most cases, it is the subculture's stylistic innovations which first attract the media's attention. Subsequently deviant or "anti-social" acts—vandalism, swearing, fight-

---

18 *Kerrang! magazine,* March 27, 1993; see also Michael Moynihan and Didrik Søderlind, *Lords of Chaos,* 100–101.

ing, "animal behavior"—are "discovered" by the police, the judiciary, the press; and these acts are used to "explain" the subculture's original transgression of sartorial codes. In fact, either deviant behavior or the identification of a distinctive uniform (or more typically a combination of the two) can provide the catalyst for a moral panic.[19]

The moral panic that followed the church burnings illustrates how easily such a scene is vilified and labeled "Satanic." Subcultures are largely imagistic and operate on the level of surfaces: Never mind that half the members of the bands involved are or were serving prison terms for their actions. A movement as such quickly becomes regarded as exclusively stylistic. Attaching Satan to a movement that was largely nationalist in nature is a move that occurs on the surface of the phenomenon. Dayal Patterson points out that black metal "will surely continue to innovate and evolve, and this should be celebrated."[20] Once it reached the shores of the States, the bands there show how far this style has spread since its spiked-leather beginnings.

A Looming Resonance[21]

In America, where history is always already lost to the self-same spectacle encroaching on Norway, black metal seeks not a return to any sort of nationalism, but a return to the

---

19 Dick Hebdige, *Subculture: The Meaning of Style* (New York: Routledge, 1979), 93.

20 Dayal Patterson, *Black Metal: The Evolution of the Cult* (Port Townsend, WA: Feral House, 2013), 484.

21 Wolves in the Throne Room, "A Looming Resonance," from *Malevolent Grain* [EP], Los Angeles: Southern Lord, 2009.

wilderness, to introspection, away from media and technology. Borrowing everything from the Scandinavians except the panda paint, American black metal bands blend the core aesthetic with other subgenres to great effect, the most notable and widespread being the rising and falling structures of post-rock and the ambient guitar squalls of shoegaze. All of these subgenres are about meditation, contemplation, and intro-spection, in sharp contrast to the pomp and posturing of their rock 'n' roll forebears. Over the past several years, this melding and welding of metal has become my favorite accompanying sound for almost any activity. Its energy, its all-encompassing crests and crumbles, its sheer power moves me in ways no other genre has in many years. And I am not alone: The dark-ness of this stuff touches something in us, something buried deep in our beings, in our nature.

Among the best of this mix of subgenres stateside are Washington state's Wolves in the Throne Room and Califor-nia's Deafheaven. The former's Cascadian black metal is as majestic as it is monolithic, mixing the forest and the trees. Their epic songs can be as dense as they are sparse. Their explanation of the draw of black metal from a 2006 interview is worth quoting at length:

> True Norwegian black metal is completely unbalanced – that is why it is so compelling and powerful. It is the sound of utter torment, believing to one's core that winter is eternal. BM [black metal] is about destruction, destroy-ing humanity; destroying one's own self in an orgy of self-loathing and hopelessness. I believe one must focus on this image of eternal winter in order to understand black metal for it is a crucial metaphor that reveals our sadness and woe as a race. In our hubris, we have rejected the earth

Back to Nature: Wolves in the Throne Room. Photo by Peter Beste

and the wisdom of countless generations for the baubles of modernity. In return, we have been left stranded and bereft in this spiritually freezing hell.

To us, the driving impulse of black metal is more about deep ecology than anything else and can best be understood through the application of eco-psychology. Why are we sad and miserable? Because our modern culture has failed – we are all failures. The world around us has failed to sustain our humanity, our spirituality. The deep woe inside black metal is about fear – that we can never return to the mythic, pastoral world that we crave on a deep sub-conscious level. black metal is also about self-loathing, for modernity has transformed us, our minds, bodies and spirit, into an alien life form; one not suited to life on earth without the mediating forces of technology, culture and organized religion. We are weak and pitiful in our strength over the earth – in conquering, we have destroyed our-selves. black metal expresses disgust with humanity and revels in the misery that one finds when the falseness of our lives is revealed.[22]

The urge to return to our roots is a prevailing ethos in black metal of all paints. In Norway, it's about returning to the Norse traditions that predate the Western influences on the culture there. For Wolves in the Throne Room, it's about a return to nature. "Our music is balanced in that we temper the blind rage of black metal with the transcendent truths of the universe that reveal themselves with age and experience," they continue. "Our relationship with the natural world is a healing force in our lives."[23] Drummer and one half of the brothers that make up the core of Wolves in the Throne Room, Aaron Weaver was taken by black metal upon first hearing it.

It's more about creating a trance effect. It's really got more in common with shamanic drumming and with noise music. It's not heavy metal, it's not riffs, it's not head-bang-

22 Quoted in Bradley Smith, "Interview with Wolves in the Throne Room," *Nocturnal Cult*, 2006, http://www.nocturnalcult.com/WITTRint.htm.

23 Ibid.

ing music at all… It's meditative music. Most heavy metal is very extroverted. It's about putting on a big show and head banging and drinking a beer with your buddies. Black metal is the exact opposite. It's all about gazing inwards and trying to discover things about yourself.[24]

Their music is introspective to the point of turning one inside out. "The real truth hidden in black metal is a call to completely destroy the world. […] I'm talking about destroying the world on a spiritual level."[25]

Weaver discusses the connections between black metal and the radical Northwestern culture he and his brother are immersed in, both of which are about "critiquing civilization, yearning for a more ancient sense of the world, a connection with tradition and nature that we've perhaps lost as modern people."[26] Considering themselves largely apolitical, their ideology has been described as "ecoanarchism." That's not the whole of it, of course. He adds,

Then the darker side of it as well exists in both worlds. In both the black metal world and the ecological punk world, a hatred of humanity and a strong sense of misanthropy as we look around and see what humanity has wrought.[27]

---

24 Quoted in Matthew Moyer, "Wolves in the Throne Room: From Mount Olympia," *Ghettoblaster*, no. 30, Winter 2011, 42.

25 Quoted in Andrew Parks, "Wolves in the Throne Room Profile," *Decibel Magazine*, April 2009, 20.

26 Quoted in Moyer, "Wolves in the Throne Room," 42.

27 Ibid.; see also Timothy Morton, "At the Edge of the Smoking Pool of Death: Wolves in the Throne Room," *Helvete: A Journal of Black Metal Theory* 1 (Winter 2013): 21–28.

Rotten with Perfection: *Sunbather*-era Deafheaven.
Photo by Reid Haithcock, 2013

Where Wolves in the Throne Room want to reverse the damage done by humanity by returning to earlier times, Deafheaven withdraws further into the self. Their break-out 2013 record, *Sunbather*, describes a decidedly human situation. "The record surrounds the feeling of longing for perfection and the frustration and sadness of knowing that it can never be achieved," says vocalist George Clarke.[28]

"You might come across American black metal and see a greater tendency to humanize the terms, which may seem somewhat contradictory," says He Who Crushes Teeth from Deafheaven's California neighbors, Bone Awl, "But I think an unknown goal in American black metal is to level the vocabulary and draw attention to the fact that nothing is outside of humanity."[29] The rhetorical critic Kenneth Burke defined the human as

---

28 Quoted in Jason Heller, "Deafheaven Profile," *Decibel Magazine*, August 2013, 32.

29 Quoted in Brandon Stosuy, "Meaningful Leaning Mess," in *Hideous Gnosis: Black Metal Theory Symposium 1*, ed. Nicola Masciandaro

the symbol using, making, and mis-using animal, inventor of the negative, separated from his natural condition by instruments of his own making, goaded by the spirit of hierarchy, and rotten with perfection.[30]

The very Burkean phrase "rotten with perfection" is an apt description of *Sunbather*, not only in its intent but also in its execution. "The 'Sunbather' is essentially the idea of perfection," Clarke tells *National Underground*,

a wealthy, beautiful, perfect existence that is naturally unattainable and the struggles of having to deal with that reality because of your own faults, relationship troubles, family troubles, death, etc.[31]

Balancing ambitions for more with an appreciation for what we have is a definitively human struggle. Wanting to transcend those limits and find out what's beyond them is human as well.

Localizing Hell

Touted by some as the "Scariest Music in the World,"[32] Stalaggh, and later Gulaggh, went to the very home of humanity's limits for their sounds: the asylum. The "gh"

(Lexington, KY, 2012), 152.

30 Kenneth Burke, *Language as Symbolic Action* (Berkeley, CA: University of California Press, 1966), 16.

31 Quoted in Anthony Glaser, "Interview: Deafheaven," *National Underground*, March 11, 2013, http://nationalunderground.org/2013/03/11/interview-deafheaven/.

32 See https://www.bitchute.com/video/zhsk3HVz5btd/.

suffix in their name stands for "global holocaust" because that's what they were trying to set off, like some sort of a planet-spanning Helter Skelter.[33] Named after the P.O.W. camps in Nazi Germany (Stalag) and the rehabilitation and labor camps in the former Soviet Union (Gulag), they told Brandon Stosuy of *Pitchfork*, "our name represents the total annihilation of human life."[34] They continue,

> Black metal made people burn churches and kill people and terrorize in the name of intolerance. Music *can* cause chaos and fear. People into gothic, ambient, electro music have an overall depressed and dark state of mind. They are generally *not* averse to suicide. They are into auto-mutilation. We consider this a good start, but it is only a beginning. They should be on all fields motivated to more radical actions, against both themselves and other human beings. We want people to feel miserable and depressed.[35]

Stalaggh and Gulaggh were made up of several unnamed members of Dutch and Belgian black metal bands who set out to make the most oppressive music possible, topped with the vocals of criminally insane mental patients

---

33 See Jerome Reuter, "Stalaggh/Gulaggh: A Window into Suffering and the Necessity for Transgressive Art," *Diabolique Magazine*, November 15, 2020, https://diaboliquemagazine.com/stalaggh-gulaggh-a-window-into-suffering-and-the-necessity-for-transgressive-art/.

34 Quoted in Brandon Stosuy, "Show No Mercy," *Pitchfork*, June 20, 2007, https://pitchfork.com/features/show-no-mercy/6633-show-no-mercy/.

35 Ibid.

— screams allegedly belonging to a man who murdered his own mother by stabbing her thirty times and to another man who committed suicide soon after the recording was over. "We decided that a normal black metal vocalist was not what we were looking for," they say.

> The pain and hate in the vocals must be real, not acted. We needed humans with a real mental illness. Only someone in constant mental pain or with a homicidal aggression could provide the vocals for our Audio-Terror.[36]

"Art is creative, we are destructive." Stalaggh: The faces of Global Holocaust

---

36 Ibid.

"For thousands of years human beings have tried to localize hell," Verge (Bruno Ganz) explains in Lars von Trier's 2018 movie *The House That Jack Built.*

Among other methods by seeking the sound it generates. One shouldn't focus on extracting screams and wailing because the cries of pain of so many millions of individuals together becomes what you have just heard: a buzzing sound whose intensity will increase as we get ever closer to the presence of suffering.[37]

Verge is Jack's guide, à la Dante Alighieri's *Inferno*, through his thoughts and deeds, to the afterlife of the underworld. Throughout the film, the titular Jack (Matt Dillon) is attempting to construct a house. He is an engineer, not an architect. As to the difference, he explains to one of his victims, "An engineer reads music; an architect plays music." Jack is also a serial killer.

"The art of engineering is first and foremost about statics," he says. "That is so things remain standing in spite of the various forces that impact the buildings." Jack reduces the engineering problems of his house to the material used in its construction: "I often say that the material does the work. In other words, it has a kind of will of its own, and by following it, the result will be the most exquisite." During this discussion, he mentions Hitler's architect, Albert Speer, and Speer's use of both strong and weak materials in his buildings so that a thousand years later they would

---

37 Lars von Trier (writer and director), *The House That Jack Built* [motion picture] (Hvidovre, Denmark: Zentropa Entertainments, 2018).

leave behind "aesthetically perfect ruins." Like the three little pigs, Jack tries bricks, wood, and other conventional building materials to no avail. "Find the material, Jack," Verge says, "and let it do the work."[38]

Jack stashes his victims' bodies in a large, walk-in freezer space. After experimenting with them, he finds he can twist them into new poses, pose them into new scenes. At Verge's urging, Jack finally builds his house out of the frozen corpses of his many victims. The ideal building material ends up being dead people, human bodies used as raw materials for the most basic technology: shelter.

This Mortal Soil

The use of mental patients for something as frivolous as a black metal recording or frozen bodies as building materials might send up humanitarian red flags, but as human population continues to grow, humans are more likely to be used as a resource, raw materials for any use whatever. Moreover, the human rights in question diminish as the resources grow as well. In what Broadrick calls the "constant repetition of existence,"[39] we are the mistake that keeps on mistaking: mistaking ourselves as exceptional, mistaking ourselves as unique, mistaking ourselves as important. Even when we recognize ourselves as fallible, we still make

---

38 Ibid.

39 Quoted in Jason Heller, "Justin Broadrick of Jesu"; Douglas Coupland calls it "Strangelove Reproduction: Having children to make up for the fact that one no longer believes in the future," *Generation X: Tales for an Accelerated Culture* (New York: St. Martin's Press, 1991), 135.

more—the crumbling façades of buildings and the crumbling flesh of bodies.

Humanity doesn't scale, and human nature is a farce. People will do what people will do, but we will rarely surprise you. That complete lack of surprise is all that could be called human nature. The sad predictability of the species is its nature. As Eugene Thacker puts it, "On the one hand we as human beings are the problem; on the other hand at the planetary level of the Earth's deep time, nothing could be more insignificant than the human."[40] Where posthumanism is most often associated with the biotechnical augmentations of cyborgs discussed before, fixing us up rather than following after we've gone, this is the posthumanism of extinction.[41]

In Alan Weisman's 2007 book, *The World Without Us*, which speculates what life on Earth will like after humans cease to exist, he describes us as senders rather than receivers of signals, and that radio waves dispatched and drifting through space will be our final legacy. The human brain is also a transmitter, broadcasting electric impulses at very low frequencies that some believe can be focused to exact

40 Thacker, *In the Dust of This Planet*, 158.

41 Daniel Lukes, "Black Metal Machine: Theorizing Industrial Black Metal," *Helvete: A Journal of Black Metal Theory* 1 (Winter 2013): 71–73; see also Cary Wolfe, *What Is Posthumanism?* (Minneapolis, MN: University of Minnesota Press, 2009); and Jussi Parikka, "Planetary Memories: After Extinction, the Imagined Future," in *After Extinction*, ed. Richard Grusin (Minneapolis, MN: University of Minnesota Press, 2018), 27–49.

actions at a distance. "That may seem far-fetched," Weisman writes, "but it's also a definition of prayer."[42]

On a more grounded note, David Leo Rice writes,

Absurd as this hope surely is, I wonder if there might be a grain of truth in it. Since we, too, are creatures of the earth, made of earthly materials (as are our digital devices), perhaps there is something in our nature that can reach beyond our limited time as humans, and partake in the larger cycle of dust returning to dust. Perhaps some part of the consciousness of the earth itself exists within us, and will go on existing.[43]

---

42 Alan Weisman, *The World Without Us* (New York: St. Martin's Press, 2007), 274.

43 Rice, "The Overlook Hotel"; he continues, "To believe this is to believe in an afterlife of time, rather than space: to believe that human consciousness, once it has become disembodied, will not travel upward or downward to heaven or hell, nor into space as radio waves, but rather that it will linger here on earth, as earth, even when that earth is transformed into a planet that, if we were to perceive it while still human, would have to be called alien. This is the dream of the entire species being present at its own funeral." As Roberts puts it, "The end is final, and yet it also represents a strange new beginning"; Adam Roberts, *It's the End of the World, But What Are We Really Afraid of?* (London: Elliott & Thompson Limited, 2020), 9; see also Timothy Morton, *Ecology Without Nature: Rethinking Environmental Aesthetics* (Cambridge, MA: Harvard University Press, 2010).

Weak transmitters, antennae for sound, or just sentient meat, however we seek a way beyond them, we are bound by our bodies: malleable yet mortal, elastic yet earthbound. We are soil as much as we are souls.[44] The dust of this planet is people.[45]

---

44 As William Bryant Logan writes, "Human bodies belong to and depend on dirt. We spend our lives hurrying away from the real, as though it were deadly to us. But the soil is all of the earth that is really ours." *Dirt: The Ecstatic Skin of the Earth* (New York: Riverhead, 1995), 97.

45 Like much of the rest of this book, this final line owes its existence to both McKenzie Wark and Eugene Thacker. It combines and pays homage to the last lines of McKenzie Wark, *Dispositions* (Cromer, UK: Salt Publishing, 2002), and Eugene Thacker, *In the Dust of This Planet*.

9

AFTERWORD

A Chance of Pain

"One day you might find cause to ask yourself what the limit is to some pain you're experiencing, and you'll find out there is no limit at all. Pain is inexhaustible. It's only people that get exhausted."
— Ray Velcoro, *True Detective*[1]

"Pain's a secret no one keeps."
— Publicist UK, "Levitate the Pentagon"[2]

"Pain looks great on other people.
That's what they're for."
— The Sisters of Mercy, "Wrong"[3]

If there's anything that will bring you hurtling back to your body, it's physical pain, a ready reminder that your physical form is inescapable. Even so, pain is intoxicating. We seek it out. We can't live without it. It makes us feel alive in a way that nothing else does. Happiness, elation, ecstasy, excitement,

---

1   Nic Pizzolatto (writer), *True Detective* [television series] (New York: HBO, 2014).

2   Publicist UK, *Forgive Yourself* [LP] (Los Angeles: Relapse, 2015).

3   The Sisters of Mercy, *Vision Thing* [LP] (Los Angeles: Elektra, 1990).

contentment—these feelings are elusive and fleeting. Pain is certain and ready at hand whenever we need it.

After a bicycle wreck in the busy streets of Chicago years ago, I spent several weeks in a leg brace and the first two weeks of those on crutches. The experience slowed me down in many ways, not all of which were bad. I'm not recommending cracking a kneecap to get reacquainted with the everyday, but a good jarring of the sensorium might help us all once in a while. Nothing brings reality crashing back in like crashing back into reality.

In addition to my patella, I also broke my phone. The cracking of its screen left it useless for texting or taking pictures. Ironically, the only thing it would do was send (provided I knew or could find the number) and receive calls. I also stopped wearing headphones as my injury already made me an easy mark. These two things—no texting and no headphones—reconnected me with aspects of my days I'd been avoiding or ignoring.

Also, I had to change up my commute. For one thing, I obviously wasn't able to ride my bike to work, which is what I was doing when I crashed. I wasn't able to take the train, because I lived almost a mile from the closest station and I couldn't walk that far on crutches. It should also be noted that there are only a few Chicago Transit Authority train stations with elevators. Stairs were out of the question for a few weeks. This put me on a multiple-bus-route commute that took me through parts of Chicago I'd never seen.

Possibly the most important factor that made breaking my kneecap an enlightening experience was sociological rather than technological. Collectively, we tend to *other* the impaired among us. That is, there seems to be a clear delineation between the impaired and the normal; however, if one of us is only temporarily injured, we sympathize, empathize, or pity them.

In the month that I wasn't texting or listening to music and had a bum leg, I had countless uplifting and informative conversations with people whom I wouldn't have spoken to otherwise and who wouldn't have spoken to me for one reason or the other. All of the above made me feel far more connected to my fellow humans than any technology or so-called "social" media.

My smashing my knee into the pavement at the origami triangle fold of traffic that is the intersection of Elston, Fullerton, and Damen in Chicago shoved me out of my comfort zone in several ways. One thing I noticed on my temporarily revised, much-longer commute to campus was a lot of needless anger: a man walking by the bus stop, angry at his dog for being a dog; a lady with her children, angry at them for being children; people on the bus, angry about being on the bus; the bus driver, angry about the people on the bus; and on and on. I wasn't exactly happy that my right patella was fractured in two places. I certainly had good and bad days recovering, and I'm not better than any of those mentioned above, but I tried to smile at everyone, laugh at my fumbling around on crutches, do my work, and generally let others carry the anger. Getting out of your comfort zone doesn't have to be quite so uncomfortable, but sometimes being forced is the only way for it to happen. It felt like I needed it.

With that said, a physical therapist saw me out hobbling down the sidewalk in Logan Square with my leg brace on one day. He stopped and asked me about my injury with genuine and professional interest. He then informed me that a broken patella is the most painful kind of injury, which, he added, is supposedly why it is the chosen punishment for those late on their loan or gambling payments. I don't recommend getting behind.

Pain is an early warning system, a physical sign of something larger gone awry.

Illicit Metabolism

"I've had minimal drug experiences because of fear," says the artist Peter Gabriel. "I can trust machines, yet I can't trust pills… A machine you can always switch off or get out of… whereas when a pill gets hold of your metabolism, you have to ride through."[4] Pain is the counterpoint. You either ride out the pain or you ride out a drug to relieve the pain. But as David Cronenberg reminds us, "we absorb all technologies into our bodies." Drugs aside, we have to metabolize more and more of our machines.

"Body is reality," reads the catchphrase for Cronenberg's *Crimes of the Future*. The writer and director says that the film "is about the crimes committed by the human body against itself." He says it's "a meditation on human evolution […] the ways in which we have had to take control of the process because we have created such powerful environments that did not exist previously."[5] He goes on to ponder,

At this critical junction in human history, one wonders — can the human body evolve to solve problems we have created? Can the human body evolve a process to digest

---

4   Quoted in Daryl Easlea, *Without Frontiers: The Life and Music of Peter Gabriel* (London: Overlook Omnibus, 2014), 152.

5   Quoted in Angel Melanson, "'A Meditation on Human Evolution' *Crimes of the Future* Redband Trailer Is Here!" *Fangoria*, May 6, 2022, https://www.fangoria.com/original/a-meditation-on-human-evolution-crimes-of-the-future-redband-trailer-is-here/.

plastics and artificial materials not only as part of a solution to the climate crisis, but also, to grow, thrive, and survive?[6]

Channeling his former teacher Marshall McLuhan, Cronenberg reminds us,

Technology is always an extension of the human body, even when it seems to be very mechanical and non-human. A fist becomes enhanced by a club or a stone that you throw — but ultimately, that club or stone is an extension of some potency that the human body already has.[7]

We don't tend to think of our technologies as an environment. We don't tend to think that we're reshaping ourselves—and our bodies—with every new contrivance. In his introduction to *Crash*, J.G. Ballard wrote that "what our children have to fear is not the cars on the highways of tomorrow but our own pleasure in calculating the most elegant parameters of their deaths."[8] Warning labels and warding spells: a future defined by risk assessment models and worst-case scenarios.

---

6   Ibid.

7   Quoted in Clark Collis, "Kristen Stewart Gets the Body Horror Treatment in the New Teaser for David Cronenberg's *Crimes of the Future*," *Entertainment Weekly*, April 14, 2022, https://ew.com/movies/crimes-of-the-future-trailer-viggo-mortensen-kristen-stewart/.

8   Quoted in Paul March-Russell, "How writing about JG Ballard's most controversial novel helped me cope with becoming a single parent," *The Independent*, September 22, 2024, https://www.the-independent.com/voices/jg-ballard-crash-single-parent-children-b2616926.html.

While pain connects us to our own flesh, it isolates us from others. To have pain is to be certain of your physical existence, to be certain of your living and being, and to be certain of your mortality. To have pain is to be alone in your body.

Mythology of Self

"I'm here to express the pain I feel," Justin Broadrick says in a 2023 interview with *Decibel Magazine*, "and I don't take much pleasure in that at all."[9] There is a pain inherent to life, the pain of existence. To many of us, to be alive is to suffer.

Godflesh has always induced a furious form of suffering on their listeners, and a lot of Broadrick's music comes from some severe shade of anxiety. After years of self-medicating with drugs and alcohol, which only made it worse, he was diagnosed with autism and PTSD at fifty-two years old. With that revelation, he was finally able to properly deal with his mental health, decades of compounded pain eased with new tools for coping and care.

"I've spent a lifetime trying to please everyone, to make myself feel comfortable," he says, "a lifetime of not doing things because I'm uncomfortable. Now I'm not masking it so much anymore."[10] On "Nero," from 2023's hip-hop beat-infused *Purge*, he barks, "Restrain yourself/ Betray/ Your needs," and on "Land Lord" he says, "Bad seeds/ Own you/ Shape you/ Slay you/ Control/ Divide/ Enslave/ Destroy."[11] If ever his lyrics were masking his discomfort, they certainly aren't anymore. Bassist Benny Green adds,

---

9   Quoted in Daniel Lake, "Long May I Dream These Nightmares," *Decibel Magazine*, July 2023, 56.

10 Quoted in Lake, "Long May I Dream These Nightmares," 58.

11 Godflesh, *Purge* [LP]. (London: Avalanche Recordings, 2023).

Our general abhorrence at the monstrous injustices humans have always inflicted on each other still impacts us to this day. We'd both quite happily hide away in a remote forest or cave in order not to have to deal with the horrors of mankind.[12]

He finds solace in the sonorous: "For me, music, sound, tone, whatever you want to call it," he continues, echoing Robert Fludd's idea of a celestial monochord, "is the single most powerful and liberating thing there is, and the whole universe exists through vibrations and waves, music included."[13] Call it Godflesh, an all-encompassing energy that connects us all, each to another and beyond.[14]

---

12 Quoted in Lake, "Long May I Dream These Nightmares," 60.

13 Ibid.

14 Jane Bennett writes, "According to Spinoza's theory of bodies, all bodies are modes of a common substance, which can be called either God or Nature."; Jane Bennett, Vibrant Matter (Durham, NC: Duke University Press, 2010), 117–118.

Acknowledgements

When Godflesh's first full-length record came out on November 13, 1989, I was just out of high school. In an issue of *SPIN Magazine* at the time, Faith No More's Mike Patton described *Streetcleaner* as the sound of your Walkman's batteries running down. That was enough of an endorsement for me to seek out the record. As well versed as I was in the metal of the time, what I found was like nothing I'd ever heard.

So first, I have to thank Justin K. Broadrick. I first met Justin in late November of 1996 when Godflesh played Seattle on what was to be their last US tour until they reunited two decades later. I was the editor of *Pandemonium! Magazine*, Tacoma, Washington's own music monthly, which had just gone out of business, and I'd just put Godflesh on the cover of our final issue the month before.

I was on my way out the door for a job interview when the phone rang. It was the publicist at Earache Records, Godflesh's label at the time. She wanted to know if I knew anyone who could give the guys a ride to their in-store appearance at Cellophane Square in the U-district that afternoon before the show that night at the Fenix Underground. I distinctly remember my voice cracking as I said, "I could do that!"

All I was thinking during my interview was that I was going to pick up Godflesh right after. I couldn't remember the questions or my answers as I drove to their hotel in my 1983 Honda Civic hatchback. I was wearing a button-up shirt and a tie, and as Justin climbed into my tiny car he asked, "How was your interview?"

Pandemonium! Magazine, no. 47, October 1996.
Cover design by J. Matthew Youngmark

We spent that whole day together. He signed records for a line of fans, and we shopped for hip-hop CDs. Then we headed to the Fenix for soundcheck, dinner, and then the show. I didn't see Justin again until Jesu toured with Isis eleven years later in 2007. I was back in Seattle then. I took a bus up to Neumo's on Capitol Hill. As I was walking up the sidewalk on Pike, I spotted Justin hanging out the side door talking to two other dudes. When I approached, he said, "Hey, I know you—Roy!"

We've managed to stay in touch over all these years, through Godflesh, Jesu, Final, Godflesh again, and his countless other projects. It's because of Justin's art and friendship that this book exists, and he provided invaluable insight as I was writing it.

Many thanks to the early readers of this material, including Gary J. Shipley, Peter Bebergal, B.R. Yeager, Robert Guffey, Eugene Thacker, Aaron Weaver, Michael Schandorf, Scott Heim, Steven Shaviro, Rick Moody, Alex Burns, David Barker, Nicole NeSmith, and Claudia Dawson for their insightful comments and kind words. Thanks to Mark Dery for his generous and insightful Foreword. Dery's 1996 book *Escape Velocity* was this one's original namesake (*Escape Philosophy*, punctum books, 2022) and should be considered one of its parents. Thanks to Chloë Manon at the Graveface Museum, Jeni Lambert at Earache Records, Mike Sullivan of Russian Circles, Trevor de Brauw of Pelican, Stephanie Marlow, Peter Beste, Reid Haithcock, Alap Momin, Will Brooks, Mike Manteca, John Mohr, J. Robbins, Kim Coletta, Bill Barbot, Dominic Pettman, McKenzie Wark, Josh Gunn, Alyssa Byrkit, James Ward Byrkit, and Spike Jonze for their help with images, facts, and general encouragement. Thanks to Howard Rheingold, Erik Davis, and Shane Mauss for answering my drug questions. Thanks to Godflesh, Jawbox, Deafheaven, Wolves in the Throne Room, Celtic Frost, and Stalaggh for inspiration.

Special thanks to Lily Brewer, whose many thoughtful comments and insightful edits made this the book that it is. Michael Grasso also deserves special mention for helping extensively during the initial writing and editing process. Thanks also to Tariq Goddard, Josh Turner, Johnny Bull, Carl Neville, Christopher DeVeau, and Vicky Hartley at Repeater Books past and present.

Finally, extra special thanks to my coauthor and companion Korra Dog and to Anondi King for changing everything.

Discography

Agent Orange. *This is the Voice* [LP]. Los Angeles: Enigma Records, 1986.

Ain, Martin Eric. "A Dying God Coming into Human Flesh." On *Monotheist* [LP]. Recorded by Celtic Frost. Dortmund: Century Media Records, 2006.

Catherine Wheel. "Black Metallic." On *Ferment* [LP]. Los Angeles: Fontana, 1992.

Deafheaven. *Infinite Granite* [LP]. Los Angeles: Sargent House, 2021.

Deafheaven. *New Bermuda* [LP]. Los Angeles: Anti-, 2015.

Deafheaven. *Ordinary Corrupt Human Love* [LP]. Los Angeles: Anti-, 2018.

Deafheaven. *Roads to Judah* [LP]. Beverly: Deathwish, Inc., 2013.

Deafheaven. *Sunbather* [LP]. Beverly: Deathwish, Inc., 2013.

Fall of Because. *Life is Easy* [CD]. Chicago: Invisible Records, 1999.

Godflesh. *A World Lit Only by Fire* [LP]. London: Avalanche Recordings, 2014.

Godflesh. *Hymns* [LP]. London: Music for Nations, 2001.

Godflesh. *Godflesh* [EP]. London: Silent Scream, 1988.

Godflesh. *Post Self* [LP]. London: Avalanche Recordings, 2017.

Godflesh. *Pure* [LP]. London: Earache Records, 1992.

Godflesh. *Purge* [LP]. London: Avalanche Recordings, 2023.

Godflesh. *Selfless* [LP]. New York: Columbia, 1994.

Godflesh. *Streetcleaner* [LP]. London: Earache Records, 1989.

Godflesh. *Streetcleaner: Live at Roadburn 2011* [LP]. Roadburn Records, 2013.

Greymachine. *Disconnected* [LP]. Los Angeles: Hydra Head Records, 2009.

Gulaggh. *Vortuka* [LP]. New Era Productions, 2008.

Head of David. *Dustbowl* [LP]. London: Blast First, 1988.

Head of David. *White Elephant* [LP]. London: Blast First, 1989.

Isis. "In Fiction." On *Panopticon* [LP]. Los Angeles: Ipecac Records, 2012.

Jesu. *Conqueror* [LP]. Los Angeles, Hydra Head Records, 2007.

Jesu. *Heartache & Dethroned* [EP]. Los Angeles: Hydra Head Records, 2010.

Jesu. *Jesu* [LP]. Los Angeles: Hydra Head Records, 2004.

Jesu. *Pale Sketches* [LP]. Avalanche Recordings, 2007.

JK Flesh. *Posthuman* [LP]. 3by3 Music, 2012.

Manic Street Preachers. "Mausoleum." On *The Holy Bible* [LP]. New York: Epic Records, 1984.

Milemarker. "Insect Incest." On *Sex Jams* [7" single]. New Gretna: Bloodlink Records, 1999.

Miller, Daniel. "T.V.O.D." On "Warm Leatherette" [7" single]. Recorded by The Normal. London: Mute Records, 1978.

Napalm Death. *Scum* [LP]. London: Earache Records, 1986.

Open Mike Eagle. *Brick Body Kids Still Daydream* [LP]. Tucson: Mello Music Group, 2017.

Publicist UK. *Forgive Yourself* [LP]. Los Angeles: Relapse, 2015.

Robbins, J. "Motorist." On *Jackpot Plus* [7" single]. Recorded by Jawbox. Washington, DC: Dischord Records, 1993.

Siousxie and the Banshees. "Night Shift." On *Juju* [LP]. London: Polydor, 1981.

Siouxsie Sioux & Budgie. "Miss the Girl." On *Feast* [LP]. Recorded by The Creatures. London: Polydor, 1983.

The Sisters of Mercy. *Vision Thing* [LP]. Los Angeles: Elektra, 1990.

Stalaggh. *Nihilistik Terror* [CD]. New Era Productions, 2006

Stalaggh. *Projekt Misanthropia* [CD]. Autopsy Kitchen Records, 2007.

Stalaggh. *Projekt Nihil* [LP]. New Era Productions, 2003.

Stalaggh. *Projekt Terror* [LP]. Total Holocaust Records, 2004.

Stalaggh. *Pure Misanthropia* [LP]. New Era Productions, 2008.

Tears for Fears. "Mad World." On *The Hurting* [LP]. New York: Mercury Records, 1983.

Wolves in the Throne Room, "A Looming Resonance," on *Malevolent Grain* [EP] (Los
Angeles: Southern Lord, 2009).

Wolves in the Throne Room. *Black Cascade* [LP]. Los Angeles: Southern Lord, 2009.

Wolves in the Throne Room. *Celestial Lineage* [LP]. Los Angeles: Southern Lord, 2011.

Wolves in the Throne Room. *Thrice Woven* [LP]. Olympia: Artemsia Records, 2017.

Wolves in the Throne Room. *Primordial Arcana* [LP]. Philadelphia: Relapse Records, 2021.

Wolves in the Throne Room. *Two Hunters* [LP]. Los Angeles: Southern Lord, 2007.

Filmography

Ambrose, David, and Richard Fleischer, dirs. *Amityville 3-D*. Los Angeles: Orion Pictures, 1983.

Barron, Steve, dir. *Electric Dreams*. Written by Rusty Lemorande. Los Angeles: Virgin Films, 1984.

Brahm, John, dir. *The Twilight Zone*. Season 1, episode 8, "Time Enough at Last," written by Rod Sterling, starring Burgess Meredith. Aired November 20, 1959, on CBS.

Byrkit, James Ward, dir. *Coherence*. Brooklyn: Oscilloscope Laboratories, 2013.

Cronenberg, David, dir. and writer. *Crash*. Los Angeles: Universal Pictures, 1996.

Cronenberg, David, dir. and writer. *Crimes of the Future*. Los Angeles: Decal, 2022.

Cronenberg, David, dir. and writer. *Videodrome*. Montreal: Alliance Communications, 1983.

Ducournau, Julia. dir. and writer. *Titane*. Paris: Kazak Productions, 2021.

Dunn, Sam, and Scott McFadyen, creators. *Metal Evolution*. Toronto, Canada: Banger Films, 2011.

Jones, Duncan, dir. and writer. *Moon*. Los Angeles: Sony Pictures Classics, 2009.

Kelly, Richard, dir. and writer. *Donnie Darko*. Los Angeles: Newmarket, 2001.

Kelly, Richard, dir. and writer. *Southland Tales*. Los Angeles: Universal, 2006.

Lumet, Sidney, dir. *Network*. Written by Paddy Chayefsky. Los Angeles: Metro-Golden-Mayer, 1976.

Pizzolatto, Nic, writer. *True Detective*. New York: HBO, 2014.

Russell, Ken, dir. *Altered States*. Los Angeles: Warner Bros., 1980.

von Trier, Lars, dir. and writer. *The House That Jack Built*. Hvidovre: Zentropa Entertainments, 2018.

Bibliography

"The Shedding of Our Borrowed Human Bodies May Be Required in Order To Take Up Our New Bodies Belonging to the Next World." *HeavensGate.com*, August 18, 1994. https://heavensgate.com/book/611.htm.

Accius, Lucius. *Atreus. Archive of Performances of Greek & Roman Drama*. 140–86 BCE. http://www.apgrd.ox.ac.uk/ancient-performance/performance/809.

Adams, Richard. *Watership Down, A Novel*. London: Rex Collings, 1972.

Alexander, Chris. "The Skin He's In." *Fangoria Magazine*, no. 322, May 2014, 42–46.

Anselmi, J.J. *Doomed to Fail: The Incredibly Loud History of Doom, Sludge, and Post Metal*. Los Angeles: Rare Bird Books, 2020.

Balch, Robert W., and David Taylor. "Salvation in a UFO." *Psychology Today* 10, no. 5 (October 1976): 58–60.

Ballard, J.G. *The Atrocity Exhibition*. London: Jonathan Cape, 1970.

Ballard, J.G. *Crash: A Novel*. London: Jonathan Cape, [1973] 1985.

Ballard, J.G., *Extreme Metaphors: Collected Interviews*, edited by Simon Sellars and Dan O'Hara. London: Fourth Estate, 2012.

Ballard, J.G. *High-Rise: A Novel*. London: Jonathan Cape, 1975.

Barad, Karen. *Meeting the Universe Halfway: Quantum Physics and the Entanglement of Matter and Meaning*. Durham: Duke University Press, 2007.

Barker, Martin, Jane Arthors, and Ramaswami Harindranath. *The Crash Controversy: Censorship Campaigns and Film Reception*. London: Wallflower Press, 2001.

Bartkewitcz, Anthony. "Vision: Escape: Justin Broadrick." *Decibel Magazine*, March 2007, 68–74.

Baumgarten, Marjorie. "Sitting in a Tin Can, Where Hell Is Still Other People: Director Duncan Jones on his debut film, 'Moon.'" *The Chronicle*, July 10, 2009. https://www.austinchronicle.com/screens/2009-07-10/808103/.

Beck, Don, and Christopher Cowan. *Spiral Dynamics: Mastering Values, Leadership, and Change*. New York: Wiley-Blackwell, 1996.

Bennett, Jane. "Q&A with Justin Broadrick." *Decibel Magazine*, January 2011, 40–42.

Bennett, Jane. *Vibrant Matter: A Political Ecology of Things*. Durham, NC: Duke University Press, 2010.

Berardi, Franco "Bifo." *Heroes: Mass Murder and Suicide*. New York: Verso, 2015.

Beste, Peter. *True Norwegian Black Metal: We Turn in the Night Consumed by Fire*. New York: Vice Books, 2008.

Bhattacharya, Sanjiv. "Scarlett in Bloom," *New York Magazine*, February 5, 2004: https://nymag.com/nymetro/shopping/fashion/spring04/n_9843/

Bohme, Johannes. "An Interview with Rem Koolhaas." *The Believer*, January 31, 2020.

Bolton, Lucy. "'Under the Skin' and the Affective Alien Body." In *Film-Philosophy Conference 2014: A World of Cinemas*. January 2014.

Bradbury, Ray. *The Illustrated Man*. New York: Doubleday, 1951.

Bradbury, Ray. *The Martian Chronicles*. New York: Doubleday, 1950.

Bradshaw, Peter, Deyan Sudjic, Dave Simpson, Iain Sinclair, and Mark Lawson. "How J.G. Ballard Cast His Shadow Right Across the Arts." *The Guardian*, April 20, 2009. https://www.theguardian.com/books/2009/apr/20/jg-ballard-film-music-architecture-tv.

Braidotti, Rosi. *Nomadic Subjects: Embodiment and Sexual Difference in Contemporary Feminist Theory*. New York: Columbia University Press, 1994.

Braidotti, Rosi. *The Posthuman*. Cambridge: Polity, 2013.

Bratton, Benjamin. *The Stack: On Software and Sovereignty*. Cambridge: MIT Press, 2015.

Brown, David Jay. "From Here to Alterity and Beyond with John C. Lilly." In *Mavericks of the Mind: Conversations for the New Millennium*, edited by David Jay Brown and Rebecca McClen Novick, 203–225. Berkeley: The Crossing Press, 1993.

Brown, Norman O. *Life Against Death: The Psychoanalytical Meaning of History*. Middletown: Wesleyan University Press, 1959.

Brummett, Barry. *Contemporary Apocalyptic Rhetoric*. New York: Praeger, 1991.

Burke, Kenneth. *Language as Symbolic Action: Essays on Life, Literature, and Method*. Berkeley: University of California Press, 1966.

Burnett, Joseph. "Extreme Language: An Interview with Justin K. Broadrick." *The Quietus*, May 9, 2012. https://thequietus.com/interviews/jk-flesh-interview-justin-broadrick/.

Burroughs, William S. *Naked Lunch*, New York: Grove Press, 1959.

Butler, Judith. *Gender Trouble: Feminism and the Subversion of Identity*. New York: Routledge, 1990.

Butler, Judith. *Precarious Life: The Powers of Mourning and Violence*. New York: Verso, 2004.

Calia, Michael. "Writer Nic Pizzolatto on Thomas Ligotti and the Weird Secrets of 'True Detective.'" *Wall Street Journal*, February 2, 2014. https://www.wsj.com/articles/BL-SEB-79577.

Card, Claudia. *The Atrocity Paradigm: A Theory of Evil*. New York: Oxford University Press, 2002.

Chang, Alvin. "Every Mass Shooting in the US – A Visual Database." *The Guardian*, June 2022. https://www.theguardian.com/us-news/ng-interactive/2021/may/27/us-mass-shootings-database.

Chayefsky, Paddy. *Altered States: A Novel*. New York: HarperCollins, 1978.

Christopher, Roy. "Godflesh: Heads Ain't Ready." *SLAP Skateboard Magazine*, December 1997, 77.

Christopher, Roy. "Godflesh: Uneasy Listening." *Pandemonium! Magazine*, October 1996, 22–23.

Cimino, Al. *Ted Bundy: America's Most Evil Serial Killer*. London: Arcturus, 2021.

Clark, Andy. *Natural Born Cyborgs: Minds, Technologies, and the Future of Human Intelligence*. New York: Oxford University Press, 2003.

Clarke, George L. *Westlake and Selected Writings*. Los Angeles: Sargent House, 2017.

Clover, Carol J. *Men, Women, and Chain Saws: Gender in the Modern Horror Film*. Princeton: Princeton University Press, 1992.

Condon, Edward. *Final Report of the Scientific Study of Unidentified Flying Objects*. New York: Dutton, 1969.

Connole, Edia. "Seven Propositions on the Secret Kissing of 333 Black Metal: OSKVLVM." In *Mors Mystica: Black Metal Theory Symposium*, edited by Edia Connole and Nicola Masciandaro. London: Schism, 2015.

Connor, Steven. *Dumbstruck: A Cultural History of Ventriloquism*. Oxford: Oxford University Press, 2000.

Copenhaver, Brian R., trans. *Corpus Hermeticum*. Cambridge: Cambridge University Press, 1992.

Coupland, Douglas. *Generation X: Tales for An Accelerated Culture*. New York: St. Martin's Press, 1991.

Crane, Leah. "Elon Musk Demonstrated a Neuralink Brain Implant in a Live Pig." *NewScientist*, August 29, 2020. https://www.newscientist.com/article/2253274-elon-musk-demonstrated-a-neuralink-brain-implant-in-a-live-pig/.

Cronin, Claire. *Blue Light of the Screen: On Horror, Ghosts, and God*. London: Repeater Books, 2020.

Cross, Roger. *The Yorkshire Ripper: The In-Depth Study of a Mass Killer and his Methods*. London: HarperCollins UK, 1981.

Davis, Erik. *High Weirdness: Drugs, Esoterica, and Visionary Experience in the Seventies*. London: Strange Attractor, 2019.

Davis, Erik. *Techgnosis: Myth, Magic, and Mysticism in the Age of Information*. New York: Harmony, 1998.

Davis, Erik. "Terrence McKenna's Last Trip." *WIRED*, May 1, 2000. https://www.wired.com/2000/05/mckenna/.

Davis, Susan E., & Demello, Margo. *Stories Rabbits Tell: A Natural and Cultural History of a Misunderstood Creature*. New York: Lantern Books, 2003.

Davis, Wade. *The Serpent and the Rainbow*. New York: Touchstone, 1985.

de Certeau, Michel. *The Practice of Everyday Life*. Berkeley: University of California Press, 1984.

Delgado, José M.R. *Physical Control of the Mind: Toward a Psychocivilized Society*. New York: Harper & Row, 1969.

Denzler, Brenda. *The Lure of the Edge: Scientific Passions, Religious Beliefs, and the Pursuit of UFOs*. Berkeley: University of California Press, 2001.

Dery, Mark. *Escape Velocity: Cyberculture at the End of the Century*. New York: Grove Press, 1996.

Dery, Mark. *The Pyrotechnic Insanitarium: American Culture on the Brink*. New York: Grove Press, 1999.

Dick, Philip K. *Flow My Tears, the Policeman Said*. New York: Doubleday, 1974.

Dolar, Mladen. *A Voice and Nothing More*. Cambridge: The MIT Press, 2006.

Douglas, Mary. *Implicit Meanings: Essays in Anthropology*. London: Routledge & Keegan Paul, 1975.

Douglas, Mary. *Purity and Danger: An Analysis of the Concepts of Pollution and Taboo*. London: Routledge & Keegan Paul, 1966.

Douglas, Mary. *Natural Symbols: Explorations in Cosmology*. London: Barrie & Rockliff, 1970.

Duncan, John. *The Error*, curated by Simone Menegoi. Prato: Galleria Enrico Fornello. April 15–June 17, 2006. Exhibition.

Dyens, Ollivier. *Metal and Flesh: The Evolution of Man: Technology Takes Over*. Translated by Evan J. Bibbee and Ollivier Dyens. Cambridge: The MIT Press, 2001.

Ebert, Roger. "Review of 'Crash' (1997)." *RogerEbert.com*, March 21, 1997. http://www.rogerebert.com/reviews/crash-1997. Archived at https://web.archive.org/web/20200805084346/https://www.rogerebert.com/reviews/crash-1997.

Ferrante, Garth. "Godflesh Explains 'Selfless''s Song Titles." *Godflesh.com*, August 1994. https://godflesh.com/articles/int2.txt.

Fisher, Mark. *The Weird and the Eerie*. London: Repeater Books, 2016.

Fludd, Robert. "On the Occult and Wondrous Effects of Secret Music." In *Tractatus Apologeticus Integritatum Societatis de Rosea Crucis defendens*. Leiden, 1617.

Foster, Maureen. *Alien in the Mirror: Scarlett Johansson, Jonathan Glazer and* Under the Skin. Jefferson, NC: McFarland, 2019.

Fuller, Curtis G. *Proceedings of the First International UFO Congress.* New York: Warner Books, 1980.

Galbraith, John Kenneth. *The New Industrial Society.* London: Hamish Hamilton, 1967.

Giannopoulos, Stavros. Artist on Artist: Deafheaven. *B-Side.* July 4, 2015, B6-B7, B9.

Gibson, Andrew. *Misanthropy: The Critique of Humanity.* New York: Bloomsbury Academic, 2017.

Glaser, Anthony. "Interview: Deafheaven." *National Underground,* March 11, 2013. http://nationalunderground.org/2013/03/11/interview-deafheaven/.

Glenn, Jerome C., and Theodore J. *Futures Research Methodology, V2.0.* Washington, DC: AC/UNU Millennium Project, 2003.

Gorman, John. "Tanking." *OMNI Magazine,* August 1980, 61-64.

Gould, Stephen Jay. *Questioning the Millennium: A Rationalist's Guide to a Precisely Arbitrary Countdown.* New York: Crown, 1999.

Green, Ryan. *Trust Me: The True Story of Confession Killer Henry Lee Lucas.* Independently published, 2019.

Guffey, Robert. *Chameleo: A Strange but True Story of Invisible Spies, Heroin Addiction, and Homeland Security.* New York: O/R Books, 2015.

Gunn, Joshua. *Modern Occult Rhetoric: Mass Media and the Drama of Secrecy in the Twentieth Century.* Tuscaloosa: University of Alabama Press, 2005.

Hamilton Helle, Una, and Lotte Brown. *Becoming the Forest.* 3 vols. Antwerp: Het Bos, 2015-2019.

Haraway, Donna J. *Simians, Cyborgs, and Women: The Reinvention of Nature.* New York: Routledge, 1990.

Hayes, Linda (writer) & Wolfinger, Lisa Quijano (director). *Wild Crime:* "Season 2: Murder in Yosemite." Los Angeles: Hulu. October 25, 2022.

Hayles, N. Katherine. *How We Became Posthuman: Virtual Bodies in Cybernetics, Literature, and Informatics.* Chicago: University of Chicago Press, 1999.

Hebdige, Dick. *Subculture: The Meaning of Style.* New York: Routledge, 1979.

Heikkilä, Melissa. "Machines Can Read Your Brain. There's Little That Can Stop Them." *Politico,* August 31, 2021. https://www.politico.eu/article/machines-brain-neurotechnology-neuroscience-privacy-neurorights-protection/.

Heim, Michael. *The Metaphysics of Virtual Reality.* Oxford: Oxford University Press, 1993.

Heim, Michael. *Virtual Realism.* Oxford: Oxford University Press, 1998.

Heller, Jason. "Deafheaven Profile." *Decibel Magazine,* August 2013, 32.

Heller, Jason. "Justin Broadrick of Jesu." *AV Club,* April 5, 2007. https://film.avclub.com/justin-broadrick-of-jesu-1798211103.

Hofstadter, Douglas. *Fluid Concepts and Creative Analogies: Computer Models of the Fundamental Mechanisms of Thought.* New York: Basic Books, 1995.

Hofstadter, Douglas, and Daniel C. Dennett. *The Mind's I: Fantasies and Reflections on Self and Soul.* New York: Bantam, 1981.

Hollinger, Veronica. "A History of the Future: Notes for an Archive." *Science Fiction Studies,* 37, no. 1 (March 2010): 23–33. https://www.jstor.org/stable/40649583.

Hooper, Judith. "Interview: John Lilly." *OMNI Magazine,* January 1983, 57–58, 74–82.

Horsley, Jonathan. "Justin Broadrick Interview: Godflesh, Growing Up and Anarcho-Punk. *Decibel Magazine*, October 7, 2011. http://www.decibelmagazine.com/featured/justin-broadrick-interview-godflesh-growing-up-and-anarcho-punk/.

Howell, Linda. "The Cyborg Manifesto Revisited: Issues and Methods for Technocultural Feminism." In *Postmodern Apocalypse: Theory and Cultural Practice at the End*, edited by Richard Dellamora, 199–218. Philadelphia: University of Pennsylvania Press, 1995.

Howells, Tom. *Black Metal: Beyond the Darkness*. London: Black Dog Publishing, 2012.

Itzkoff, David. *Mad as Hell: The Making of Network and the Fateful Vision of the Angriest Man in Movies*. New York: Times Books, 2014.

James, William. *The Varieties of Religious Experience: A Study in Human Nature*. New York: Random House, 1994.

Jansen, Karl. *Ketamine: Dreams and Realities*. San Jose: MAPS, 2001.

Jastrow, Robert. *The Enchanted Loom: Mind in the Universe*. New York: Simon & Schuster, 1984.

Johnson, Alex. "Between God and Flesh." *Thora-Zine*, 9, 1995.

Jones, Barbara. *Voices from an Evil God: The True Story of the Yorkshire Ripper and the Woman Who Loved Him*. London: Blake Publishing, 1993.

Joy, Bill. "Why the Future Doesn't Need Us." *WIRED*, no. 8.04. April 2000, 238–262.

Jouve, Nicole Ward. *"The Streetcleaner": The Yorkshire Ripper Case on Trial*. London: Marion Boyars, 1986.

Jung, Carl G. *Flying Saucers: A Modern Myth of Things Seen in the Skies*. Princeton: Princeton University Press, 1978.

Jung, Carl G. *Man and His Symbols*. New York: Bantam, 1964.

Kelly, Richard. *The Donnie Darko Book*. London: Faber and Faber, 2003.

Kiang, Jessica. "'Crash': The Wreck of the Century." *The Criterion Collection*, December 1, 2020. https://www.criterion.com/current/posts/7206-crash-the-wreck-of-the-century.

Knapp, Bettina. *Machine, Metaphor, and the Writer: A Jungian View*. University Park: Pennsylvania University Press, 1989.

Koczan, J.J. "Jesu Interview: Justin Broadrick Confirms New Godflesh Studio Album, Discusses Jesu's Latest, Imperfection, Self-Indulgence, Roadburn, and Much More." *The Obelisk*, May 6, 2011. http://theobelisk.net/obelisk/2011/05/06/jesuinterview/.

Koestler, Arthur. *The Roots of Coincidence: An Excursion into Parapsychology*. New York: Vintage, 1972.

Kraus, Chris. *Video Green: Los Angeles Art and the Triumph of Nothingness*. New York: Semiotext(e), 2004.

Kroker, Arthur. *Body Drift: Butler, Hayles, Haraway*. Minneapolis: University of Minnesota Press, 2012.

Kurzweil, Ray, "A Review of 'Her' by Ray Kurzweil." *Kurzweil*, February 10, 2014. https://www.kurzweilai.net/a-review-of-her-by-ray-kurzweil.

Lacan, Jacques. "Some Reflections on the Ego." *The International Journal of Psychoanalysis* 34 (1953): 11–17.

Lake, Daniel. "Long May I Dream These Nightmares: How Justin Broadrick's Evolving Enlightenment Shines in the Sonic Purge of Godflesh." *Decibel Magazine*, July 2023.

Lakoff, George. "The Contemporary Theory of Metaphor." In *Metaphor and Thought*, edited by Andrew Ortony, 202–51. Cambridge: Cambridge University Press, 1993.

Langman, Peter, ed. "Eric Harris's Journal." *School Shooters.info* (October 3, 2014).

Lanier, Jaron. *You Are Not a Gadget: A Manifesto*. New York: Alfred A. Knopf, 2010.

Lawrence, D.H. *Women in Love*. New York: Thomas Seltzer, 1920.

Lepselter, Susan. *The Resonance of Unseen Things: Poetics, Power, Captivity, and UFOs in the American Uncanny*. Ann Arbor: University of Michigan Press, 2016.

Leslie, Charles. Review of *The Ritual Process: Structure and Anti-Structure* by Victor W. Turner. *Science* 168, no. 3932 (May 1970): 702–704.

Ligotti, Thomas. *The Conspiracy Against the Human Race*. New York: Hippocampus Press, 2010.

Lilly, John C. *Programming and Metaprogramming in the Human Biocomputer: Theory and Experiments*. New York: The Julian Press, 1974.

Lilly, John C. *Simulations of God: The Science of Belief*. New York: Simon and Schuster, 1975.

Lilly, John C. *The Center of the Cyclone: An Autobiography of Inner Space*. New York: The Julian Press, 1972.

Lilly, John C. *The Deep Self: Profound Relaxation and the Tank Isolation Technique*. New York: Simon and Schuster, 1977.

Lilly, John C. *The Scientist: A Novel Autobiography*. New York: Lippincott, 1978.

Lilly, John C., and E.J. Gold. *Tanks for the Memories: Floatation Tank Talks*. Penn Valley: Gateways Books & Tapes, 1996.

Lilly, John C., and Philip Hansen Bailey Lilly. *The Quiet Center*. Berkeley: Ronin Publishing, 2003.

Lockley, R. M. *The Private Life of the Rabbit*. New York: Macmillan Publishing, 1964.

Logan, William Bryant. *Dirt: The Ecstatic Skin of the Earth*. New York: Riverhead, 1995.

Lukes, Daniel. "Black Metal Machine: Theorizing Industrial Black Metal." In *Helvete: A Journal of Black Metal Theory, Issue 1,* edited by Amelia Ishmael, Zareen Price, Aspasia Stephanou, and Ben Woodard, 69–93. Earth: punctum books, 2013.

Masciandaro, Nicola. "On the Mystical Love of Black Metal." In *Floating Tomb: Black Metal Theory*, edited by Nicola Masciandaro and Edia Connole, 101–14. Milan: Mimesis, 2015.

Maslin, Janet. "Screen: Ken Russell's 'Altered States.'" *New York Times*, December 25, 1980, Section 1, 15.

Mayakovsky, Vladimir. "A Cloud in Trousers." In *Russian Poetry: The Modern Period*, edited by John Glad and Daniel Weissbort. Iowa City: University of Iowa Press, 1978.

McKenna, Terence. *The Archaic Revival: Speculations on Psychedelic Mushrooms, the Amazon, Virtual Reality, UFOs, Evolution, Shamanism, the Rebirth of the Goddess, and the End of History*. New York: HarperCollins, 1991.

McLean, Adam. "Quantum Consciousness." *Alchemy Web Site*. https://www.alchemywebsite.com/quantum.html.

McLuhan, Marshall. *The Gutenberg Galaxy: The Making of Typographic Man*. Toronto: University of Toronto Press, 1962.

McLuhan, Marshall. *Understanding Media: The Extensions of Man*. New York: Houghton-Mifflin, 1964.

Melton, J. Gordon. "The Contactees: A Survey." In *The Gods Have Landed: New Religions from Other Worlds*, edited by James R. Lewis, 1–13. Albany: University of New York Press, 1995.

Metzner, Ralph. "John Lilly and Ketamine: Some Personal Recollections." In *The Ketamine Papers: Science, Therapy, and Transformation*, edited by Phil Wolfson and Glenn Hertelius, 47–50. San Jose: Multidisciplinary Association for Psychedelic Studies, 2016.

Michael, Chris. "Spike Jonze on Letting 'Her' Rip and 'Being John Malkovich.'" *The Guardian*. September 9, 2013. https://www.theguardian.com/film/filmblog/2013/

sep/09/spike-jonze-her-scarlett-johansson. Archived at https://web.archive.org/web/20201005152729/https://www.theguardian.com/film/filmblog/2013/sep/09/spike-jonze-her-scarlett-johansson.

Miéville, China. "Introduction." In *Miracles of Life: Shanghai to Shepperton, An Autobiography*, by J.G. Ballard, ix–xiv. New York: Liveright, 2008.

Minsky, Marvin. "Telepresence." *OMNI Magazine*, June 1980, 45–52.

Moravec, Hans. *Mind Children: The Future of Robot and Human Intelligence*. Cambridge: Harvard University Press, 1988.

Moravec, Hans. "The Senses Have No Future." In *The Virtual Dimension: Architecture, Representation, and Crash Culture*, edited by John Beckmann, 84–95. New York: Princeton Architectural Press, 1998.

Morton, Timothy. "At the Edge of the Smoking Pool of Death: Wolves in the Throne Room." In *Helvete: A Journal of Black Metal Theory Theory, Issue 1*, edited by Amelia Ishmael, Zareen Price, Aspasia Stephanou, and Ben Woodard, 21–28. Earth: punctum books, 2013.

Morton, Timothy. *Dark Ecology: For a Logic of Future Coexistence*. New York: Columbia University Press, 2016.

Morton, Timothy. *Ecology Without Nature: Rethinking Environmental Aesthetics*. Cambridge: Harvard University Press, 2010.

Moten, Fred. *Black and Blur: Consent Not to Be a Single Being*. Durham: Duke University Press, 2017.

Moyer, Matthew. "Wolves in the Throne Room: From Mount Olympia." *Ghettoblaster Magazine* 30 (Winter 2011).

Moynihan, Michael, and Didrik Søderlind. *Lords of Chaos: The Rise of the Satanic Metal Underground*. Port Townsend: Feral House, 1998.

Moynihan, Thomas. *X-Risk: How Humanity Discovered Its Own Extinction*. Falmouth: Urbanomic, 2020.

Mudrian, Albert. *Choosing Death: The Improbable History of Death Metal and Grindcore*. Port Townsend: Feral House, 2004.

Mudrian, Albert. "Godflesh's Justin Broadrick: 'I Never Feel Comfortable at Any Festival.'" *Decibel Magazine*, October 17, 2018. https://www.decibelmagazine.com/2018/10/17/godfleshs-justin-broadrick-i-never-feel-comfortable-at-any-festival/.

Mudrian, Albert. "Just Words from the Editor." *Decibel Magazine*, March 2007.

Murchie, Guy. *Music of the Spheres, Vol. 1: The Macrocosm: Planets, Stars, Galaxies, Cosmology*. New York: Dover, 1961.

Nash, Elle. *Nudes*. Ann Arbor: Short Flight/Long Drive Books, 2020.

Nasrallah, Dimitri. "Justin Broadrick: Napalm Death – Godflesh – Techno Animal – Jesu – Pale Sketcher." *Exclaim!*, September 2010. https://exclaim.ca/music/article/justin_broadrick-napalm_death-godflesh-techno_animal-jesu-pale_sketcher.

Noakes, Tim. "Under the Skin of Scarlett Johansson." *Dazed & Confused*, Spring 2014, 118–31.

Norris, Dr. Joel. *Henry Lee Lucas: The Shocking True Story of America's Most Notorious Serial Killer*. New York: Zebra, 1991.

O'Hehir, Andrew. Review "Sympathy for the Devil Worshipers: 'Until the Light Takes Us' Movie Review." *Salon*, December 7, 2009. https://www.salon.com/2009/12/07/until_the_light/

Parikka, Jussi. "Planetary Memories: After Extinction, the Imagined Future." In *After*

Extinction, edited by Richard Grusin, 27–49. Minneapolis: University of Minnesota Press, 2018.

Parks, Andrew. "Wolves in the Throne Room Profile." *Decibel Magazine*, April 2009, 20.

Pasquinelli, Matteo. *Animal Spirits: A Bestiary of the Commons.* Rotterdam: NAi Publishers, 2008.

Pasquinelli, Matteo, "Three Thousand Years of Algorithmic Rituals," *Il Tascabile*, March 15, 2021: https://www.iltascabile. com/scienze/rituali-algoritmici/

Pasulka, Diana Walsh. *American Cosmic: UFOs, Religion, Technology.* Oxford: Oxford University Press, 2019.

Patterson, Dayal. *Black Metal: The Cult Never Dies, Volume One.* London: Cult Never Dies, 2015.

Patterson, Dayal. *Black Metal: Into the Abyss.* London: Cult Never Dies, 2016.

Patterson, Dayal. *Black Metal: Prelude to the Cult.* London: Cult Never Dies, 2016.

Patterson, Dayal. *Black Metal: The Evolution of the Cult.* Port Townsend: Feral House, 2013.

Patterson, Dayal. *The Cult Never Dies MegaZine.* London: Cult never Dies, 2016.

Peak, David. "Nothing Will Have Happened: Speculation and Horror in the Anthropocene." In *Thinking Horror, Volume Two*, edited by S.J. Bagley, 198–206. Middletown: Thinking Horror, 2021.

Peak, David. *The Spectacle of the Void.* London: Schism, 2014.

Penny, Simon. *Making Sense: Cognition, Computing, Art, and Embodiment.* Cambridge: MIT Press, 2017.

Pessaro, Fred. "Big Ups: Deafheaven Pick Their Bandcamp Favorites." *Bandcamp Daily*, December 3, 2020. https://daily. bandcamp.com/big-ups/big-ups-deafheaven.

Petersen, Aage. "The Philosophy of Niels Bohr." *Bulletin of the Atomic Scientists* 19, no. 7 (1963): 8–14. DOI: 10.1080/00963402.1963.11454520.

Pettman, Dominic. *After the Orgy: Toward a Politics of Exhaustion.* Albany: SUNY Press, 2002.

Pettman, Dominic. *Look at the Bunny: Totem, Taboo, Technology.* Winchester: Zer0 Books, 2013.

Philips, Olav. *The Secret Space Age.* Kempton: Adventures Unlimited Press, 2015.

Pilkington, Mark. "In the Province of the Mind." *Frieze,* June–August 2018. https://www.frieze.com/article/what-was-inspiration-paddy-chayefskys-hallucinatory-novel.

Poscic, Antonio. "Out Demons Out." *The Wire,* April 2022, 30–38.

Prince, Stephen. *Apocalypse Cinema.* New Brunswick: Rutgers University Press, 2021.

Randle, Kevin D. *A History of UFO Crashes.* New York: Avon Books, 1995.

Raunig, Gerald. *Dividuum: Machinic Capitalism and Molecular Revolution.* New York: Semiotext(e), 2016.

Raunig, Gerald. *A Thousand Machines: A Concise Philosophy of the Machine as Social Movement.* Translated by Aileen Derieg. New York: Semiotext(e), 2010.

Realcaptainparsnips. "Their Bodies, Ourselves: Bodysnatching and the Male Gaze in 'Under the Skin.'" *Groupthink,* March 29, 2014. Archived at https://web.archive.org/web/20150222031724/http://groupthink.jezebel.com/their-bodies-ourselves-bodysnatching-and-the-male-gaz-1554476256.

Renfro, William L. *Issues Management in Strategic Planning.* Westport: Quorum Books, 1993.

Reuter, Jerome. "Stalaggh/Gulaggh: A Window into Suffering and the Necessity for Transgressive Art." *Diabolique*

Magazine, November 15, 2020. https://diaboliquemagazine. com/stalaggh-gulaggh-a-window-into-suffering-and-the-necessity-for-transgressive-art/.

Reynolds, Simon. "Godflesh *Streetcleaner.*" *Melody Maker*, October 14, 1989, 37.

Rice, David Leo. "The Overlook Hotel." *The Believer*, October 31, 2017. https://believermag.net/logger/overlook/.

Riches, Simon, ed. *The Philosophy of David Cronenberg.* Lexington: University Press of Kentucky, 2012.

Riesman, Abraham. "William Gibson Has a Theory About Our Cultural Obsession with Dystopias." *Vulture*, August 1, 2017. https://www.vulture.com/2017/08/william-gibson-archangel-apocalypses-dystopias.html.

Roberts, Adam. *It's the End of the World, But What Are We Really Afraid of?* London: Elliott & Thompson Limited, 2020.

Roberts, Adam. *Science Fiction: The New Critical Idiom.* New York: Routledge, 2006.

Rotman, Brian. *Becoming Beside Ourselves: The Alphabet, Ghosts, and Distributed Human Being.* Durham: Duke University Press, 2008.

Rubin, Peter. *Future Presence: How Virtual Reality is Changing Human Connection, Intimacy, and the Limits of Ordinary Life.* New York: HarperOne, 2018.

Rucker, Rudy. "Outer Banks & New York #1." *Rudy's Blog*, August 2, 2015. http://www.rudyrucker.com/blog/2015/08/02/outer-banks-new-york-1/.

Rucker, Rudy. *Software: A Novel.* New York: Ace books, 1982.

Rushkoff, Douglas. *Team Human.* New York: W.W. Norton, 2019.

Sacks, Oliver. *Hallucinations.* New York: Knopf, 2012.

Sager, Mike. "Fact: Five Out of Five Kids Who Murder Love Slayer." In *Revenge of the Donut Boys: True Stories of Lust,*

Fame, Survival, and Multiple Personality. New York: Thunder's Mouth Press, 2007, 103–120.

Salzberg, Sharon. "Why Buddhist Poet Ocean Vuong Practices a Death Meditation," *Tricycle*, September 3, 2022: https://tricycle.org/article/buddhist-poet-ocean-vuong/

Scarry, Elaine. *The Body in Pain: The Making and Unmaking of the World*. New York: Oxford University Press, 1985.

Schneider, Kirk J. *Horror and the Holy: Wisdom-Teachings of the Monster Tale*. Chicago: Open Court, 1993.

SCI-Arc Channel. "Bruce Sterling & Benjamin Bratton in Conversation." *YouTube*, November 5, 2018. https://www.youtube.com/watch?v=Z0__x5SG8WY.

Sellars, Simon. "Learning to Live with Aggressionless Cars." *Foreground*, April 15, 2021. https://www.foreground.com.au/transport/learning-to-live-with-aggressionless-cars/.

Selzer, Jonathan. Liner Notes. On *Streetcleaner* [LP]. New York: Earache, 2010.

Serowy, Ulrike. *Skogtatt: A Novella*. Lohmar: Hablizel, 2013.

Shakespeare, Steven. "The Light That Illuminates Itself, The Dark That Soils Itself: Blackened Notes from Schelling's Underground." In *Hideous Gnosis: Black Metal Theory Symposium 1*, edited by Nicola Masciandaro, 5–22. Lexington: CreateSpace, 2012.

Shanahan, Murray. *Embodiment and the Inner Life: Cognition and Consciousness in the Space of Possible Minds*. Oxford: Oxford University Press, 2010.

Shaviro, Steven. *Doom Patrols: A Theoretical Fiction about Postmodernism*. New York: Serpent's Tail, 1996.

Shaviro, Steven. *Post-Cinematic Affect*. Winchester: Zer0 Books, 2010.

Shaviro, Steven. "Swimming Pool." *The Pinocchio Theory*, January 29, 2004. http://www.shaviro.com/Blog/?m=200401.

Sherlock, Ben. "Long Live the New Flesh: 10 Behind the Scenes Facts about 'Videodrome.'" *Screen Rant*, August 1, 2020. https://screenrant.com/videodrome-movie-behind-scenes-facts/.

Shipley, Gary J. "Monster at the End: Pessimism's Locked Rooms and Impossible Crimes." In *True Detection*, edited by Edia Connole, Paul J. Ennis, and Nicola Masciandaro, 1–27. London: Schism, 2014.

Shipley, Gary J. *Serial Kitsch: An Epic Poem*. London: Schism, 2017.

Shipley, Gary J. *Stratagem of the Corpse: Dying with Baudrillard, a Study of Sickness and Simulacra*. London: Anthem Press, 2020.

Shipley, Gary J. "Visceral Incredulity, or Serial Killing as Necessary Anathema." In *Serial Killing: A Philosophical Anthology*, edited by Edia Connole and Gary J. Shipley, 21–37. London: Schism, 2015.

Sinclair, Upton. *Mental Radio: Does It Work, and How?* Springfield: Charles C. Thomas, 1930.

Smith, Anthony. *The Body*. New York: Walker & Company, 1968.

Smith, Bradley. "Interview with Wolves in the Throne Room." *Nocturnal Cult*, 2006. http://www.nocturnalcult.com/WITTRint.htm.

Smith, Zadie. "Sex and Wheels: Zadie Smith on J.G. Ballard's 'Crash.'" *The Guardian*, July 4, 2014. https://www.theguardian.com/books/2014/jul/04/zadie-smith-jg-ballard-crash.

Steinbeck, John. *Of Mice and Men: A Novel*. New York: Covici-Friede, 1937.

Steinke, Darcey. "Satan's Cheerleaders." *SPIN Magazine*, February 1996, 62–68

Stengers, Isabelle. *In Catastrophic Times: Resisting the Coming Barbarism*. Translated by Andrew Goffey. Ann Arbor: Open Humanities Press, 2015.

Stenzel, Wesley, "Keanu Reeves discusses the inspiration for his first novel, *The Book of Elsewhere*: 'I think about death,'" *Entertainment Weekly*, July 18, 2024: https://ew.com/keanu-reeves-discusses-first-novel-brzrkr-book-of-elsewhere-8680552

Stine, G. Harry. "The Bionic Brain." *OMNI Magazine*, July 1979, 84–86, 121–22.

Stosuy, Brandon. "Meaningful Leaning Mess." In *Hideous Gnosis: Black Metal Theory Symposium 1*, edited by Nicola Masciandaro, 143–56. Lexington, CreateSpace, 2012.

Stosuy, Brandon. "Show No Mercy." *Pitchfork*, June 20, 2007. https://pitchfork.com/features/show-no-mercy/6633-show-no-mercy/.

Stone, Allucquère Rosanne (Sandy). "Will the Real Body Please Stand Up?" In *Reading Digital Culture*, edited by David Trend, 185–98. Malden: Blackwell, 2001.

Suarez, Gary. "Voidhead: Justin Broadrick on the End of Godflesh." *Consequence*, February 9, 2015. https://consequence.net/aux-out/voidhead-justin-broadrick-on-the-end-of-godflesh/.

Svendsen, Lars. *A Philosophy of Evil*. Champaign: Dalkey Archive, 2010.

Tew, David T. ed. *Ketamine: Use and Abuse*. New York: CRC Press, 2015.

Thacker, Eugene. *Cosmic Pessimism*. Minneapolis: Univocal Publishing, 2015.

Thacker, Eugene. *In the Dust of This Planet: Horror of Philosophy, Volume 1*. Winchester: Zer0 Books, 2011.

Thacker, Eugene. *Infinite Resignation*. London: Repeater Books, 2018.

Thacker, Eugene. "Sound of the Abyss." In *Melancology: Black Metal Theory and Ecology*, edited by Scott Wilson, 179–91. Winchester: Zer0 Books, 2014.

Thacker, Eugene. *Starry Speculative Corpse: Horror of Philosophy, Volume 2*. Winchester: Zer0 Books, 2015.

Thacker, Eugene. *Tentacles Longer Than Night: Horror of Philosophy, Volume 3*. Winchester: Zer0 Books, 2015.

The Weirdnet. "Scariest Music in the World?" *BitChute*, November 1, 2017. https://www.bitchute.com/video/zhsk3HVz5btd/.

Turkle, Sherry. *Alone Together: Why We Expect More from Technology and Less from Each Other*. New York: Basic Books, 2011.

Turner, Luke. "Greymachine: Justin Broadrick and Aaron Turner United." *The Quietus*, November 18, 2009. http://thequietus.com/articles/03246-greymachine-justin-broadrick-and-aaron-turner-united.

Turner, Victor. *Dramas, Fields, and Metaphors: Symbolic Action in Human Society*. Ithaca: Cornell University Press, 1974.

Turner, Victor. *The Ritual Process: Structure and Anti-Structure*. Ithaca: Cornell University Press, 1969.

Valcic, Vuk. "Godflesh revisits 'Streetcleaner.'" *Rock-A-Rolla Magazine*, June–July 2020, 28–29.

Vale, V., and Andrea Juno, eds. *RE/Search #8/9: J.G. Ballard*. San Francisco: Re/Search Publications, 1984.

Viola, Bill. *Reasons for Knocking at an Empty House: Writings 1973–1994*. Cambridge: The MIT Press, 1995.

Virilio, Paul. *The Art of the Motor*. Minneapolis: University of Minnesota Press, 1995.

Virilio, Paul. "The Museum of Accidents." Translated by Chris Turner. *International Journal of Baudrillard Studies* 3, no. 2 (2006). https://baudrillardstudies.ubishops.ca/the-museum-of-accidents/.

von Däniken, Erich. *Chariots of the Gods*. New York: Berkeley Books, [1970] 1999.

Vronsky, Peter. *Serial Killers: The Method and Madness of Monsters*. New York: Berkeley Publishing, 2004.

Vronsky, Peter. *Sons of Cain: A History of Serial Killers from the Stone Age to the Present*. New York: Berkeley Publishing, 2018.

Vroon, P.A. "Man-Machine Analogs and Theoretical Mainstreams in Psychology." In *Current Issues in Theoretical Psychology: Selected and Edited Proceedings of the Founding Conference of the International Society for Theoretical Psychology*, edited by W.J. Baker, M.E. Hyland, H. Van Rappard, and A.W. Staats, 393–414. Amsterdam: Elsevier, 1987.

Walczak, René. "Godflesh: Strength Through Purity." *Propaganda* 19 (Fall 1992): 40–41.

Wallace-Wells, David. *The Uninhabitable Earth: Life After Warming*. New York: Tom Duggan Books, 2019.

Wark, McKenzie. *Dispositions*. Cromer: Salt Publishing, 2002.

Wark, McKenzie. *Molecular Red: Theory for the Anthropocene*. New York: Verso, 2015.

Weisman, Alan. *The World Without Us*. New York: St. Martin's Press, 2007.

Weizenbaum, Joseph. *Computer Power and Human Reason*. San Francisco: W.H. Freeman, 1976.

Wilden, Anthony. *System and Structure: Essays in Communication and Exchange*. New York: Tavistock, 1972.

Williams, Evan Calder. *Combined and Uneven Apocalypse: Luciferian Marxism*. Winchester: Zer0 Books, 2011.

Williams, Evan Calder. "The Headless Horsemen of the Apocalypse." *Hideous Gnosis: Black Metal Theory Symposium 1*, edited by Nicola Masciandaro, 129–42. Lexington: CreateSpace, 2012.

Wilson, Robert Anton. *Down to Earth*. Vol. 2 of *Cosmic Trigger*. Las Vegas: New Falcon, 1991.

Wilson, Scott. *The Politics of Insects: David Cronenberg's Cinema of Confrontation*. New York: Continuum, 2011.

Wolf-Meyer, Matthew J. *Theory for the World to Come: Speculative Fiction and Apocalyptic Anthropology*. Minneapolis: University of Minnesota Press, 2019.

Wolfe, Cary. *What is Posthumanism?* Minneapolis: University of Minnesota Press, 2009.

Woodard, Ben. *On an Ungrounded Earth: Towards a New Geophilosophy*. Earth: punctum books, 2013.

Woodard, Ben. "The Blackish Green of the Greenish Black, or, The Earth's Coruscating Darkness." *Glossator* 6 (2011): 73–87.

Woodgate, Derek, with Wayne R. Pethrick. *Future Frequencies*. Austin: Fringecore Publishing, 2004.

Zeller, Benjamin E. *Heaven's Gate: America's UFO Religion*. New York: NYU Press, 2014.

About the Authors

Roy Christopher is an aging BMX and skateboarding zine kid. That's where he learned to turn events and interviews into pages with staples. He has since written about music, media, and culture for everything from books and blogs to national magazines and academic journals. He is the author of *The Medium Picture* and *Dead Precedents: How Hip-Hop Defines the Future* and the editor of *Boogie Down Predictions: Hip-Hop, Time and Afrofuturism* and the *Follow for Now* series of interview anthologies, among others. He holds a Ph.D. in Communication Studies from the University of Texas at Austin and writes regularly at *roychristopher.com*

Mark Dery is a cultural critic, essayist, and the author of *Escape Velocity*, a critique of the libertarian-bro ideology that dominated the Digital Revolution of the '90s, and two studies of American mythologies (and pathologies), *The Pyrotechnic Insanitarium: American Culture on the Brink* and the essay collection *I Must Not Think Bad Thoughts*, among other books. He popularized the concept of "culture jamming" and, in his 1993 essay "Black to the Future," coined the term "Afrofuturism."

JUSTIFY MY LOVE:

SEX, SUBVERSION, & MUSIC VIDEO

by

RYANN DONNELLY

In *Justify My Love*, Ryann Donnelly explores sex and gender in one of the most widely consumed art forms of our age — the music video.

Through an autobiographical reckoning with the author's life in a band and collaboration with past lovers, and a close analysis of the erotic iconography of music videos, *Justify My Love* tells the subversive history of this medium, from the inception of MTV in 1981 through to the 2010s.

Covering everything from Lady Gaga and Beyonce to Nine Inch Nails and George Michael, *Justify My Love* shows how subversion became mainstream, and how marginalised voices shaped some of the biggest music videos of the last thirty years.

Available from RepeaterBooks.com

COLLAPSE FEMINISM

THE ONLINE BATTLE FOR FEMINISM'S FUTURE

ALICE CAPPELLE

In such times of crisis, women are more likely to see their rights attacked, their sexuality scrutinised. On social media, it is claimed that women are responsible for the downfall of Western society. To make matters worse, this anti-feminist discourse has merged with internet culture and is being pushed by the algorithm into users' social media feeds.

Covering everything from the reactionary politics of the "manosphere" to sexual liberation, hookup culture, traditional femininity, the girlboss, and self-help content, *Collapse Feminism* looks at how this conservative backlash is being orchestrated online and why we must fight against it. Reversing our contemporary catastrophism, Alice Cappelle asks readers to join her and others in building a future that will liberate us all.

Order online from RepeaterBooks.com

QUIT EVERYTHING

INTERPRETING DEPRESSION

FRANCO "BIFO" BERARDI

Depression is rife amongst young people the world over. But what if this isn't depression as we know it, but instead a reaction to the chaos and collapse of a seemingly unchangeable and unliveable future?

In *Quit Everything*, Franco Berardi argues that this "depression" is actually conscious or unconscious withdrawal of psychological energy and a dis-investment of desire that he defines instead as "desertion". A desertion from political participation, from the daily grind of capitalism, from the brutal reality of climate collapse, and from a society which offers nothing but chaos and pain. Berardi analyses why this desertion is on the rise and why more people are quitting everything in our age of political impotence and the rise of the far-right, asking if we can find some political hope in desertion amongst the ruins of a world on the brink of collapse.

Order online from RepeaterBooks.com

STEAL AS MUCH AS YOU CAN

HOW TO WIN THE CULTURE WARS
IN AN AGE OF AUSTERITY

NATHALIE OLAH

Austerity has created suffering for millions, as well a generation beset with financial insecurity and crisis. Yet our TV, film, music, art and literature have never looked so rich, or so posh. During a period of immense struggle, the experiences of the majority have been pushed to the margins of our collective culture by the legacy media and its satellite industries – making it hard, if not impossible, to challenge those in power.

Steal as Much as You Can is the story of how this happened, exploring the rise of affluence in mainstream storytelling, and the corrosive effects of neoliberal and postmodern culture. By rejecting the established routines of achieving prosperity – and encouraging us to steal what we can from the establishment routes along the way – it offers hope to a bright and brilliant generation whose potential has suffered under these circumstances.

Order online from RepeaterBooks.com

REPEATER BOOKS

is dedicated to the creation of a new reality. The landscape of twenty-first-century arts and letters is faded and inert, riven by fashionable cynicism, egotistical self-reference and a nostalgia for the recent past. Repeater intends to add its voice to those movements that wish to enter history and assert control over its currents, gathering together scattered and isolated voices with those who have already called for an escape from Capitalist Realism. Our desire is to publish in every sphere and genre, combining vigorous dissent and a pragmatic willingness to succeed where messianic abstraction and quiescent co-option have stalled: abstention is not an option: we are alive and we don't agree.